MW00961909

Cracking the Code on Travel

The Ultimate Guidebook to Planning and Booking Your Trips for Less

By David Adler, founder and CEO of The Travel Secret

Disclaimer: Please note that some of the tools, tips, and tricks I will be sharing in this book work for me now and in the US, in US dollars. That doesn't mean they will work for you if you live somewhere else, and you will have to figure in the conversion rate for your currency.

Table of Contents

Introduction

Do you love to travel and wish you could afford to travel more? If you said yes, then the secrets I'm going to share with you here will blow your mind and open up a whole new world of possibilities for you in regard to travel.

In this book, I will give you over 120 of my best secrets to help you:

- Get the best deals on flights, hotels, and rental cars, in the shortest amount of time

- Plan like a pro to get the most out of every trip

- Leverage technology to travel better, smarter, and with less hassle

- Use a little-known secret to access deeply discounted fares not available to the general public

- Spend more quality time and make more priceless memories with your family

- Experience cultures deeply and get the most out of every trip

Who am I to teach you all this? My name is David Adler, and I'm an avid traveler and creator of TheTravelSecret. When I was just a young kid, about twelve years old, my parents sent me to Spain to stay with some friends in a really small town called Ávila.

It's a beautiful town in the northwest part of Spain, and I was lucky enough to spend about a month there.

This time in Spain was the first time in my life that I really traveled. It was my very first vacation. It was the first time I understood the incredible feeling you get when you travel and discover a new place. Just flying across the pond for twelve hours was an experience in itself! But when I arrived, I was mesmerized by just how different everything was. It was nothing like what I was used to at home. Everything was new: the food, the sights, the sounds, how people dressed . . .

That feeling of excitement and exploration from that very first trip to Spain is something I can still recall vividly to this day, and that is the exact reason I created my system and wrote this book. I believe that everybody deserves the chance to travel well and to do it often.

Right now, maybe more than ever, we could all use a great trip. We're tired of being stuck at home and having to cancel our vacations. We're ready to start traveling and to start planning trips for this year and beyond. We're ready to start making and collecting new memories.

Wherever you want to travel, one thing is for sure. This book will turn you into a real #travelhacker.

Are you ready?

Part 1: Planning

Benjamin Franklin once said: "By failing to prepare, you are preparing to fail."

This applies to everything in life, including travel. Planning out your future trips can help not only save time but also avoid stress and headaches along the way. Here are some resources that can help you organize your future trips to the tiniest detail.

Secret 1: Google Trips

Google is everywhere, and it dominates several industries globally. Unsurprisingly, it can help you with planning your future trips too, with a free service called Google Trips, which works worldwide. **Google Trips** automatically scans your Gmail account for emails related to your trips, such as tickets for flights and hotel reservations, and organizes them for you into one place.

It also shows you things to do, and it can even help you plan your day, filling it with numerous activities.

You can access it from a browser on your laptop, tablet, or mobile phone.

To access the service, visit: https://www.google.com/travel/.

Secret 2: TripIt

If, for some reason, you're not a fan of Google, you can always use the TripIt app.

TripIt is similar to Google Trips, since it works worldwide and is available for Android and iPhone. However, it also offers a couple of extra options.

Have you ever arrived at the airport just to realize that you forgot an important document like your passport, for example? I know it's happened to me – three times.

Besides organizing all your travel itineraries, TripIt also organizes all the documents you'll need for your trip. All you need to do is forward your reservations to TripIt, and it will create your master itinerary.

TripIt allows you to view things like the following, all in one place:

- confirmations

- flight itineraries

- tickets

- hotel and Airbnb bookings

- rental car reservations

- ferry tickets

- driving directions

The app also makes it simple for you to share your trip details with other people if you need someone to pick you up at the airport or train station, as well as with anyone else you want to keep informed about your trip.

Visit: https://www.tripit.com/web.

Secret 3: Roadtrippers

Who doesn't love a road trip? They can be great for family bonding or team building, since they are always filled with adventure and fun.

Well, the Roadtrippers app makes it easier than ever to have a successful road trip. The app is available for both Android and iPhone and can be used in the United States, Canada, New Zealand, and Australia.

The app helps you organize an epic road trip just the way you've always wanted by planning your driving route as well as finding and booking hotels along the route. It's great for finding interesting, off-the-beaten-path places, cool restaurants, and breathtaking spots that you can bookmark and go back to during the trip.

Visit: https://roadtrippers.com/.

Secret 4: Visit a City

Visit a City is available on iOS and Android. It helps solve two common challenges related to trip planning:

- figuring out how long you need to spend at each place

- maximizing your vacation time by grouping nearby attractions together

When you select a destination, the app offers recommended sightseeing guides based on the number of days you are planning to spend there.

For example, three months ago I was visiting Miami for a business conference. I selected the destination and length of stay (three days) and was given four itinerary options: Top Attractions, Family Plan, Packed Itinerary, and Easy Going.

The app automatically puts nearby attractions together and lets you know how far apart they are (e.g., three minutes by walking). It also includes the estimated time you'll spend at each place.

You can edit the itinerary by changing the day when you visit a place, revising the amount of time you spend there, or simply deleting some attractions.

Note that you'll almost certainly have to do some editing, as the itineraries don't include lunch or coffee breaks – that is, if you don't forget to eat (which happens to me when I'm amazed by the place I am visiting).

You can also book tours through the app and get general travel information about the destination, such as the best time of year to visit or tips for saving money.

The best part is that on the mobile app version, you can download the itinerary and access it offline no matter where you are in the world.

Visit: https://www.visitacity.com/.

Part 2: Packing

If you have traveled at least once in your life, there's no reason for me to tell you how important packing is. The bottom line is that you want to be well prepared for your trip by packing appropriately, which means bringing everything you need, not packing unnecessary stuff, and, of course, choosing the right luggage to pack your stuff.

My Favorite Packing Apps

Tired of making to-pack lists on sheets of paper? It's time to leave that in the past and use the apps below that will help you pack much faster and more efficiently.

Secret 5: PackPoint

Have you ever gone on a trip just to find out you didn't bring enough clothes? Or maybe you didn't have the right clothes for your activities?

With the PackPoint app, you'll be able to relax and just pack items from the list. The app gives you a list of what to bring based on several factors:

- length of your trip

- weather conditions where you'll be staying

- activities you'll be doing

- whether you'll have access to laundry facilities at your destination

All you have to do is install the app and enter the necessary information, and you'll get your packing list. Also, you can edit the list by simply removing and adding items to it.

Visit: https://www.packpnt.com/.

Secret 6: Packing Cubes

This is one of my favorite discoveries, and it honestly completely transformed the way we pack and travel.

Packing cubes make it easy to keep your stuff organized, and they come in all different sizes for shirts, footwear, pants, undergarments, etc. When you pack your items into the cubes and zip them closed, it's very easy to put them in the luggage and get going.

As my family has grown, it's been super helpful to buy packing cubes in different colors for each family member. This way you know where everything is without having to go through the whole suitcase. I even have a packing cube set for dirty clothes, so whatever we need to wash goes there, and that's the only cube I take to the cleaners or laundromat. Super helpful for staying organized.

Another reason I love these is that when you arrive at your destination, it's super easy to unpack. All you have to do is take the cubes from the luggage to the drawer, and you're done! The same happens when you are packing to go home: you just zip them up and put them back in the luggage.

The system saves a ton of time, which means that you can spend more time enjoying the destination and less time packing and unpacking everywhere you go.

You can buy them at any local luggage store, department store, or, of course, Amazon, and they are not expensive.

Secret 7: How NOT to Overpack

Although packing should be an enjoyable activity which helps you anticipate your trip with positive feelings, the truth is that most people have difficulty deciding what to pack and remembering to pack all the essentials. As I mentioned earlier in the book, PackPoint comes in handy when deciding what to take, and its checklist will help you keep track and remember what you still need to pack.

But even with the assistance of the app, it's important to remind you to try to pack as lightly as possible for your trip – within reason, of course.

Why is this so important? Well, you probably know that airlines have strict weight limits for your baggage. In other words, if your suitcase is too heavy, you'll be charged a fee.

Now, you may be thinking: "How much is too much? How can I know if I overpacked?"

The weight limit depends on the country, airline, and the type of flight you're taking. To find out the exact information, you should either ask the airline directly or do a Google search. It's also important to pay close attention to how many pieces of checked baggage you're allowed to bring with you when buying your plane ticket.

To know if your suitcase is too heavy, use a luggage scale after you're done packing. You can easily buy them online at affordable prices – especially compared to the potential fees you will pay for going over the weight limit.

This advice may be obvious to some people, but you would be surprised how many travelers find themselves paying a baggage fee at the airport just because they overpacked.

Another very important tip: make sure your baggage does not exceed the dimensions allowed by the airlines. If your bag doesn't fit the dimensions, you'll have to pay the fee as well.

Here are some additional tips to help you avoid overpacking:

- Roll up your clothes to keep them tight and wrinkle-free.

- Use packing cubes to keep you organized.

- Pack only three pairs of shoes (walking shoes, sandals for hot weather, and boots for cold weather).

- pack only necessary accessories like creams, sprays, and makeup

Secret 8: The Right Luggage

Luggage choice can either make or break your trip. Have you ever seen baggage handlers loading or unloading baggage at the airport? If you have, you know what I'm talking about.

If you choose low-quality luggage, you run the risk of it breaking during the trip. For example, if your suitcase zipper breaks while you're at the airport, your clothes will fall on the dirty airport floor. And you don't want that to happen. Not to mention baggage loading . . .

Those are only a couple of examples of how using bad-quality luggage will screw you over. That's why I recommend buying only quality luggage.

When choosing which suitcase to buy, there are a few brands that are known for their quality and reliability: Away, Tumi Samsonite, and Hartmann Luggage. It's true that they are more expensive, but there's an easy way to find them at lower prices.

If you live in North America, wait for large discounts such as Black Friday. A number of department stores will give up to 60 percent off on high-quality suitcases, allowing you to buy them at the price of cheap and unreliable alternatives.

If you plan on buying your suitcase online, don't forget to read reviews, so you know exactly what you're buying. A great resource for this is https://www.eBags.com.

Many travelers also like to use a backpack for traveling as their carry-on baggage during flights. In fact, backpacks can be extremely useful for safely carrying a variety of items, including electronics such as laptops and tablets.

However, buying a backpack is slightly different than buying a suitcase. There are durable and reliable backpacks out there that are rather cheap, but they are also smaller and don't come with many bells and whistles.

On the other hand, there are also ultra-expensive backpacks that are rather large, designed to endure a lot of weight, and come with many features such as water resistance and a power bank to charge your electronics.

No matter how much money you're willing to spend on a backpack, I recommend you buy your new backpack online – preferably on a website with reliable reviews, such as Amazon or eBags. Even though there are some famous backpack brands out there that make great backpacks, you should always read the reviews to judge the backpack. Personally, I am using the Nomatic backpack. You can find it at www.nomatic.com. It works great for three-to five-day short trips, and most of the time that's the only bag I travel with.

REI (Recreational Equipment Inc.) is another company that manufactures high-quality outdoor equipment and gear of all kinds. Many travel hackers praise REI products for their high quality and durability.

To be more specific, their backpacks can survive hundreds of trips no matter the destination or itinerary. They are made from high-quality materials and built to last.

How to Never Lose Your Luggage or Backpack

You arrive at the baggage reclaim area after a long flight with layovers just to find out that your baggage is not there. Sound familiar? It's happened to me a couple of times, and it's a stressful experience, to say the least. In that kind of situation, there's always the worry that the airline lost your checked baggage or someone else took it by mistake.

To avoid this outcome and the stress that comes with it, some people like using luggage locators that are specifically designed to fly (TSA compliant) and work anywhere around the world.

Secret 9: LugLoc

There are a variety of luggage locators on the market, but my top pick is definitely LugLoc. It uses a tracker and an app to track luggage. The tracker is smaller than your hand, and you just put it inside the suitcase you want to track and use the app to monitor the location of the tracker.

LugLoc has great battery life, and it turns on and off automatically during the flight, so it's FAA/TSA/FCC-compliant. It gives you the location on a map (in case the suitcase is stolen or missing) and also alerts you with sound or vibration when your bag is headed your way at the baggage carousel.

Visit: https://lugloc.com/.

Secret 10: Trakdot Smart Luggage Tracker

Trakdot is a mobile/GSM-based luggage tracker that comes with a mobile app, and it is overall a great alternative to LugLoc. However, it also comes with Bluetooth, so you don't always have to rely on your mobile network. It also has a subtle vibration mode that tells you when you're getting closer to your luggage.

It features a smart flight mode, which automatically turns off when the plane takes off and turns on once the aircraft lands. Finally, the battery lasts for forty-eight hours, which is great for long-haul flights.

Visit: https://www.trakdot.com/.

Part 3: Saving on Flights

I find flying extremely exciting. Knowing that I'm up in the air several miles above the ground gets my adrenaline pumping.

But the problem with flying is that it also involves airlines. Dealing with them can sometimes be very stressful. Plus, they love to charge you as much as possible.

Luckily, over the years I've spent traveling, I've found some effective strategies that can help you fly smarter and cheaper.

There are several ways to save on flights, and you'll be happy to know that you can save money both before and after the flight. Interested in how to do it? Look at the tips below.

My Top Flight Search Engines

If you want to get a good deal on flights, it's essential that you use a flight search engine. It searches all the available flights within the locations and dates you specify to find you the cheapest flight available. As a matter of fact, you can choose among the cheapest, quickest, or best flights available.

There are a lot of different search engines out there, and the best three best are Kayak, Skyscanner, and Momondo. All of them do an excellent job finding you the best deal possible. However, your best bet is Momondo.

Secret 11: Momondo

In my opinion (as always) **Momondo** is *the* best flight search engine. It is trusted by millions of travelers across the world. It's not a booking website, but it searches more than a thousand airlines, online booking sites, travel agencies, search engines, and other online travel discount sites.

It also includes small, budget airlines and less-known airlines to find the lowest airfare for you.

Visit: https://global.momondo.com/.

Secret 12: Skyscanner

This app is unique and valuable because it reveals all hidden fees. **Skyscanner** should never be overlooked, since it also offers reliable price alerts and integrated frequent flyer miles.

This app almost never gets wrong information, and it's easy to navigate. On top of that, it ensures that your car rental provider doesn't overcharge for fuel. And we all know this is often a problem for travelers.

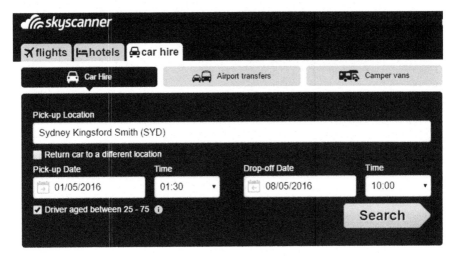

Visit: https://www.skyscanner.net/.

Secret 13: Kayak

Kayak is available both as a website and as an app for Android and iPhone. It is simple and easy to use, allowing you to compare its results to other websites such as Priceline and Expedia and suggesting nearby airports that have cheaper flights to your destination. It would take another ten pages to list all its features, but the point is that Kayak offers the best overall experience.

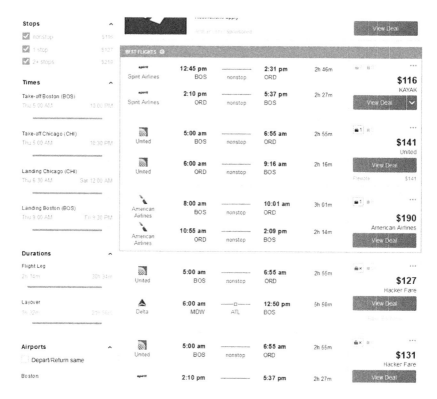

Visit: https://www.kayak.com.

Secret 14: Skiplagged

You have probably come across those online ads that offer the best-kept secrets "they" don't want you to know about. Well, that's exactly what **Skiplagged** is – one of the top secrets airline companies don't want you to know.

Skiplagged is similar to the search engines I've mentioned but with one important difference: it shows fares to connecting cities that are sometimes much cheaper than a direct flight to those places. All you have to do is book through Skiplagged, take the first flight, and then instead of taking the connecting flight, just stay at the layover location – in this case, your actual destination.

This type of discounted flight is called *hidden city ticketing,* and it isn't always available. Even when it is, there are risks associated with this strategy.

As I said, airlines don't want you to know about this strategy, and they especially don't want you to use it. If they catch you using this trick, they could take away your frequent flier miles or even ban you from the airline.

It is not a common practice for airlines to do this, but it certainly does happen. For instance, Lufthansa sued one of its passengers for using hidden city ticketing for $2,300 in 2019.

All in all, this strategy can work great, but putting it into practice is up to you and depends on how much of a daredevil you're willing to be.

Visit: https://skiplagged.com/.

Secret 15: Rome 2 Rio

Rome 2 Rio is another useful website for travelers that allows you to see how to get from one point to another cheaply. You just need to enter your departure and arrival destinations, and the website will give you all the bus, train, plane, or boat routes that can get you there, along with the prices.

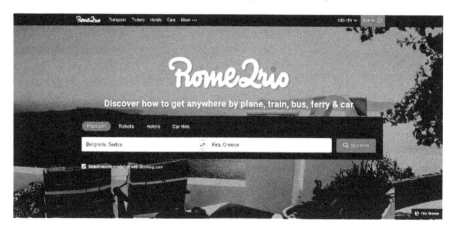

Visit: https://www.rome2rio.com/.

Secret 16: AirTreks

AirTreks can help every globetrotter save time and effort when it comes to booking flights. To be more precise, it's great for booking a multistop trip. AirTreks uses a booking engine that allows you to create itineraries with multiple airlines and thus piece together the best deals ever.

Visit: https://www.airtreks.com/.

Secret 17: Hopper

This app predicts airfare and hotel prices. It lets you predict the best time to fly, receive price alerts, and buy cheap flights in less than a minute. Seriously, **Hopper** is one of the best apps you can use to find hot travel deals.

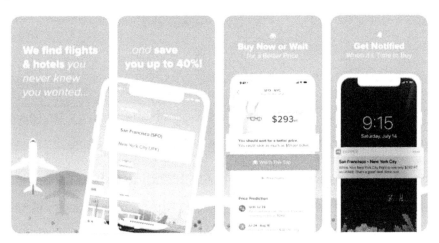

Visit: https://www.hopper.com/.

Secret 18: Getservice.com

Would you believe me if I told you that you could save over $300 on travel per year? That is exactly what **GetService** does for me.

It detects flight disruptions and hotel savings opportunities on your travel reservations and then automatically rebooks them at the lower rate. You can also use GetService to get compensation for delayed flights.

Visit: https://getservice.com/.

Priceline and Expedia are also great alternatives to those mentioned above, and they work in very similar ways.

If you're unsure which flight search engine to use, try testing them all to see which one you prefer. After a while, you will see for yourself which one gives you the best deals and overall experience.

Secret 19: Airline Reward Programs

One of the best ways to travel more and save money doing it is to use airline loyalty programs. By doing so, you can earn free tickets, free upgrades, and even free companion tickets.

The trick here is to earn points and then use them to purchase an airline ticket. Usually, you earn those points by purchasing tickets and flying with a particular airline.

No matter how frequently you fly, you should always be a part of loyalty programs, especially with the major US airlines – even if you don't live in the United States. That's because they are partners with all the major airlines in the world. This means, for example, that flying with Air France earns you points in your Delta account.

Now, earning points can be a slow process, but there is a way to earn additional points through a credit card that offers reward points for every dollar you spend on it.

That means you can purchase normal things like groceries and gas, along with things related to travel, like airline tickets, hotel rooms, and rental cars, and you will get a percentage in cash back or points. Those points or cash back can then be used for flights or other travel expenses.

Look for cards that offer additional reward points as a signup bonus, as well as higher percentages for the things you spend the most money on. Some cards offer up to 5% back on certain categories, and that can add up quickly.

The best place to find one is with a quick Google search for "airline rewards cards."

Then read the fine print carefully, so you understand how to best maximize your earnings. And, of course, pay the balance off every month, or the earnings won't mean much, because they'll be eaten up by the high interest rate you are charged.

Is Status Worth It?

Now, there are a few things to consider when earning airline miles. With most credit cards, there are different levels of discounts you can earn based on your "status" or how much you spend each year.

In my opinion, and in my situation, it is not important to try to spend more to earn a higher status. It is not going to equal more savings; rather you will just be spending more overall, and this book is about the overall bottom line.

I would rather find cheap fares and use miles for free flights than try to spend my way to status. I'm not spending $12,000, or even $6,000, a year on flights with one airline to get top-tier status.

The fact is, the vast majority of branded airline credit cards offer essentially the same perks as the lowest-level status: free checked bags, priority access, priority boarding, and discounts on in-flight food and beverages.

Strategy

Knowing that you will get basically the same basic perks with airlines, if you fly less than fifty thousand miles a year, you can fly a variety of airlines and just sign up for the loyalty programs with them all to enjoy the benefits.

However, if you fly very frequently, over fifty thousand miles a year, then loyalty programs become extremely important. In this case, I would stay loyal to one airline, because once you reach fifty thousand miles, you start getting the best perks.

If you don't think you can meet that requirement, it is better to just fly on price and save your money.

However, don't stretch yourself too widely across loyalty programs. Having a tiny balance in a lot of programs won't get you free flights and upgrades, so it is best to stick to two or three airlines that consistently have the best prices.

Also, don't hoard your points when you accumulate them, because they're a depreciating asset. Use them as soon as you have enough for the reward ticket, because you never know when the programs will change, and sometimes they expire.

Secret 20: Cookies

You might be asking yourself what the heck cookies have to do with airlines. Let me explain.

These cookies aren't the delicious cookies your grandma used to make. Cookies in this context refer to information a website stores on your computer when you visit it.

When you visit an airline's website to check the price of a ticket, they put cookies on your computer to mark that you have checked the website. Next time you check it, they use those cookies to identify you as a returning visitor and give you a higher ticket price. This applies every time you visit this website in the future.

Why on earth do they do this? Because it makes you think the price of the ticket is only increasing and that if you don't buy it as fast as possible, you will be spending more. It's an old psychological trick – using urgency to make people buy.

Luckily, there are two ways to outsmart them:

- clearing your cookies in the browser

- using Incognito Mode to browse

Clearing Cookies

You can clear your cookies on Chrome, Firefox, Safari, or any other browser. Just google "how to clear cookies" for your specific browser.

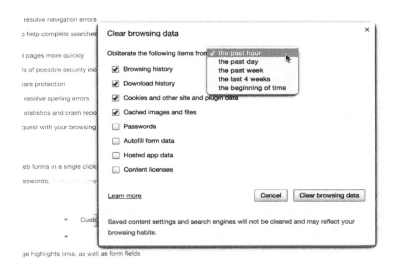

Incognito Mode

Using Incognito Mode also tackles the cookie issue because it doesn't save any cookies in the first place. All major browsers have Incognito Mode, so you should be able to use it easily.

Secret 21: VPN

In a nutshell, a VPN (virtual private network) is a technology used to hide your real IP address and make it look like you're browsing the internet from another location. For example, if you're in Japan, it can make you look as if you are browsing from the United States.

The reason a VPN is extremely useful for getting the best deals on flights is very simple – you get different prices depending on which country you're checking the flights from. There are many different ways to use this strategy, and my favorite one is to check the price from your destination.

For example, let's say I am interested in flying from London to Denver. I use a VPN to make myself appear to be browsing from London and check the price of a flight from London to Denver, which is $800. Then I use my VPN to check the price of the same flight as if I am in Denver (the destination), and the price of the flight is $650. That's a price difference of almost $150!

However, for this method to be effective, you should always clear your cookies before changing your location with a VPN.

There are many companies that offer VPN services, but my recommendation goes to Private Internet Access. They are a paid service, but not very expensive compared to other alternatives. The most important thing is that they are simple to use and reliable.

And even though this isn't a free option, it definitely works, and it could save you significantly more money on tickets in the long run.

Secret 22: Be Flexible with Travel Dates

Unless your arrival and return dates are extremely important, I recommend that you be flexible. This is because certain days are cheaper than others. For example, changing your arrival date by a single day and your departure date by two days could make a huge difference in how much you pay.

Checking for this is especially easy with flight search engines. Let's use Kayak for this demonstration.

As you can see in the image below, I searched for a flight from Las Vegas to New York and selected the arrival and departure dates. The blue dates are the ones I selected, the green ones are the cheapest, the yellow ones are more expensive, and the red ones are the most expensive.

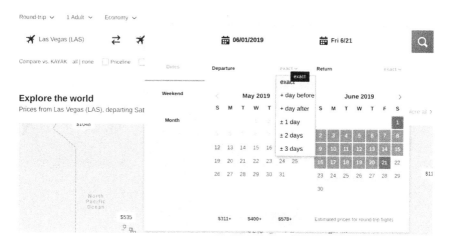

You can also select exact arrival and departure dates or make them flexible for up to a few days earlier or later. When you select a more flexible arrival and departure date, Kayak will show you the lowest prices within that time period.

However, it's not just the day you fly, but also the time of year, that will affect pricing. If you want to fly during busier periods such as Christmas, you will have to pay more. With that in mind, try to schedule your travels for less popular times of the year if possible.

Secret 23: Be Flexible with Destinations

At first, this may seem strange. However, I don't mean change your destination, but change the airport.

For this example, let's go back to Kayak and our trip from Las Vegas to New York (JFK Airport). As you can see, I searched for the flight on Kayak, and above the search results, Kayak told me there were cheaper airports nearby.

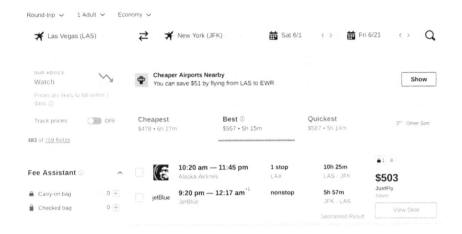

In this case, Kayak suggested that our arrival should be at Newark Airport instead of JFK, and that doing so would save us $51. A quick Google search showed us that a car ride from Newark Airport to New York City is only thirty minutes.

If you're going to rent a car anyway, you're only spending an extra half hour to save $50. But even if you're not planning to rent a car, there are still a variety of cheap options to get you to NYC, such as taking an AirTrain or shuttle services.

My point here is that busier airports are more expensive, but that doesn't mean you have to pay more. So pay attention when Kayak suggests cheaper flights at nearby airports, and be flexible.

This works all over the world. I am particularly familiar with Italy, where I used to go a lot for work. Most of the big cities in Italy have two airports, and usually, flying to the "smaller" one is cheaper, as that is the one the low-cost airlines normally use. Milan has Malpensa (the big international one) and Linate (the smaller, low-cost option). So really, being flexible does not mean traveling to another place, just choosing the right airport to fly into for the city you are looking to go to.

Secret 24: One Ticket at a Time

A lot of people who travel in pairs or larger groups buy their tickets together. And while doing so may seem easier, it will also make you pay more for your flight.

Airlines always use the highest ticket price in a group of tickets to calculate the total ticket price. If you're in a group of three, the airline will find three seats together.

Let's say that seat 1 is $170, seat 2 is $380, and seat 3 is $200. The airline will charge $380 for each individual ticket. That means that instead of paying $750, you will pay $1,140, which is a difference of $390 for the exact same flight.

The solution to this problem is simple: just search and buy your tickets separately instead of buying them together.

Secret 25: Early . . . but Not Too Early

A lot of people know that buying an airplane ticket too close to the flight date can be rather expensive. But what they don't know is that buying those tickets too early will also make them pay more.

Luckily, there's a sweet spot – a period of time when that ticket will be the cheapest. This is usually six to eight weeks before your departure or around three months before it if you're going to your destination in the peak season.

Secret 26: Getting a Refund/Compensation

Have you ever had a flight delayed or canceled? It has happened to me so many times. I remember when my flight from New York City to Belgrade was canceled, and I had to stay in New York for the night. Luckily, NYC is the city that never sleeps, so I had a great time there. But what if I was stuck in a dull place where there was nothing to do?

Well, **AirHelp** can help you with that. If your flight was in the EU or it used an EU airline, they can seek compensation from the airline for you.

All you have to do is check if your flight was eligible and provide the necessary documents, and AirHelp will take care of it for you. You don't need to deal with lawyers, spend time filling out complicated forms, or stress. AirHelp does all the hard work for you.

It also has user guides showing you how to seek compensation from your airline in other situations, like in the case of missing baggage and so on.

Visit: https://www.airhelp.com/.

Some of the best alternatives to AirHelp include Skycop and ClaimCompass, both of which are reliable and credible companies with a proven track record of helping flyers receive compensation for canceled or delayed flights.

Secret 27: Get a System That Aggregates Searches

Being able to catch an airfare deal at a discounted price is hard, almost impossible, in fact. Let me tell you why.

About twenty years ago, airlines took away all margins and commissions for agencies and took control of their pricing directly.

When they did this, they effectively eliminated the chance for third-party systems or vendors to discount tickets or work the prices. They basically removed the effectiveness of a middle man, and now they control the pricing directly.

Like you've probably realized by now with my other secrets, airlines now adjust pricing on the go, so depending on when you are booking, how you are booking, and where you are doing it from, you might get a different price.

On any given day there are over one hundred thousand flights scheduled by airlines all over the world. And most airlines use "dynamic pricing," which means the cost of flights can change for any number of reasons.

Most of the time, they change in an attempt to beat their competitors, but with so many moving parts and lightning-fast changes, mistakes happen.

Sometimes airlines publish super-cheap fares accidentally, and sometimes they aggressively slash the prices in an attempt to win back customers. However, you never really know where they post these fares.

In fact, you could find a price for a specific flight and then come back five minutes later to a completely different rate. That's how unpredictable pricing is nowadays. But don't worry, the tips in this section can help, and this secret is the best for getting a great deal. Here's how it works:

If you are like most people, when buying tickets for a flight, you have a specific destination in mind, and you look on different airfare search websites like Google Flights or Skyscanner, try different date ranges, check out the prices with different airlines, and so on. Then, the next day, you go through another round of research, hoping to find that specific route for less.

That is how I used to search for an airline ticket as well.

However, I started facing some challenges. In order to find an airfare ticket at a super-low price, I had to do two things:

First, I had to do all this endless research and book months in advance, and second, I had to keep my eyes wide open all the time and jump from site to site like crazy.

One day, I had had enough of it. I realized that spending twenty plus hours hunched over my laptop for a 20 percent discount just wasn't fair.

And at that very moment, it dawned on me . . .

What if I could get the lowest-priced airfare for my destination, from every website out there, instantly at the click of a single button?

I decided to invest time and money to build a system that does exactly that. It aggregates all the flight prices from hundreds of vendors into one simple-to-use page.

When I shared this with a few friends, they begged me to try it. Some of them even offered me money so they could access it.

The system is part of the amazing **TheTravelSecret** program that I created, and I'll tell you a bit more further in the book, because the system works for everything: hotels, cars, cruises, activities, and even travel insurance. Here I'm going to show you the benefits of using it for flights. If you want to see what it's all about, you can find it here: http://www.thetravelsecret.com/.

When you sign up and go to the Flights section, you can search just like you do on any other site: enter your departure and destination airports and the specific dates and hit Search.

Then the magic happens . . .

The system will automatically go to the biggest airlines vendors and bring back the best price available to you at the moment of your search. That way you don't have to spend hours and hours searching online. It's a simple click, click, and boom, the best price is in front of you. A true gamechanger!

Secret 28: Bonus Tip for All Cruise Lovers

If you like to roam the oceans, **TheTravelSecret** is also your best bet. Why? Because the system has access to what are called *net rates*, which means it gives you the bottom line base price offered by the cruise line at the time of your search. Also, because of TheTravelSecret's relationship with the biggest cruise lines in the world, they are able to get special pricing on cruise deals that are not offered anywhere else on the web.

In fact, many travelers claim that they have found a cruise as cheap as thirty bucks a night on the site. And to be honest, that's very hard to beat.

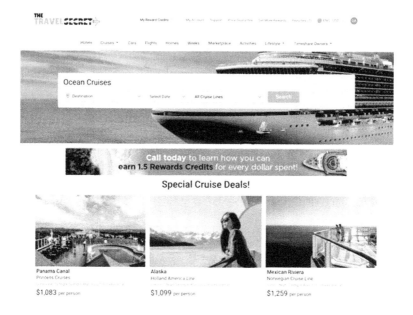

Visit: https://www.thetravelsecret.com.

Flying in Style

Flying is sometimes associated with unpleasant situations, crowds of people, and long waiting times. But it doesn't have to be like that all the time.

If you want your flying experience to be more comfortable and with less hassle, here are some resources that will help you fly in style.

Secret 29: Chartering a Plane

Have you ever wondered what it's like to charter a private plane for yourself? I don't blame you if you have, because flying in a private jet is an extremely comfortable experience.

First, there is no need to arrive at the airport several hours in advance. In fact, you can arrive just fifteen minutes before the flight takes off.

Not to mention some of the benefits during the flight, such as extra luggage space, entertainment, dining facilities, and multimedia resources. Depending on the jet, there are even bedrooms, bathrooms, lounges, office spaces, and conference rooms.

And best of all, there are hundreds of airports in the United States alone that accept private jet traffic, so you can often fly straight to your destination without the need for layovers or long transfers.

Sure, this sounds amazing, but one question still remains: how can we afford these kinds of flights?

The most affordable way to fly on a private jet is on what's called a *leg flight*, also known as an *empty sector flight*. When a regular client of a private jet airline books a one-way flight, the airplane either has to make the return journey afterward or reposition to pick up passengers from another airport.

To avoid losing money with an empty aircraft, those return journeys are usually heavily discounted, sometimes by up to 75 percent. These types of flights are especially common during summertime in the United States, although there are deals for all year round.

The *New York Times* interviewed a woman named Rachel Raymond, who described flying on a private jet as one of the most unreal experiences of her life – a fantasy she thought she would never be able to fulfill. Rachel flew with her husband and three kids on a Cessna Citation III from Westchester County Airport in White Plains, New York, to upstate Saratoga Springs, and the flight was provided by a company called **JetSuite**. The plane came with two pilots and a well-stocked bar, and she was able to take it because she found a last-minute deal on it for only $500.

These last-minute deals for one-way private flights can cost between $500 and $2,000. JetSuite isn't the only company offering these types of deals though. Blade and JetSmarter also have special flights for all of us who aren't millionaires but want to feel like one.

When you book such a deal, you fly with a small group of other people. True, it isn't as private as having the jet all to yourself, but it's much more luxurious than a regular airline flight. Also, since those flights take off from smaller private airports, that means you don't have to deal with TSA or stand in long lines.

If you like how all this sounds, your best bet is to contact one of the private jet companies to learn more about potential discounted flights they currently offer or might offer in the future.

Secret 30: Priority Pass

Back to regular airline flights . . . More often than not, waiting for your flight at the airport can be a rather uncomfortable experience.

Luckily, **Priority Pass** was created to make things easier. It gives you access to more than a thousand lounges worldwide and provides meal vouchers at certain airport restaurants around the world.

There are two ways to get a Priority Pass membership:

- Several credit cards such as American Express Platinum Card and Chase Sapphire Reserve Card offer Priority Pass memberships for free.

- You can pay an annual membership, and depending on your membership tier, you also have to pay a fee to enter certain lounges.

Visit: https://www.prioritypass.com/.

They also offer an app to Priority Pass members, which shows you a list of lounges and restaurants you have access to, photos of the lounges, and the amenities they offer. The app is available for both Android and iPhone users.

Secret 31: Mobile Passport

You've just arrived back home from an international flight, tired and ready to get out of the airport. But there's one little problem – you still have to stand in a mile-long line to go through customs.

Guess what, if you're a US citizen, you don't have to deal with this anymore. The official app made by the US Customs and Border Protection Agency, called Mobile Passport Control, allows you to skip all the frustration. It is available on Android and iPhone smartphones, and it will save you a lot of time and stress when re-entering the country.

It's quick and easy to use, and below you can see all the steps that can help you save a lot of time when coming back from another country.

Visit: https://mobilepassport.us/.

Secret 32: Seat Alerts

Most of us have a favorite seat on a plane. Some prefer the aisle seat, others the middle seat. Me, I love the window seat because I enjoy looking at the sky while flying. Also, that way I can see my hometown way before the plane lands and get high on that feeling of coming back home.

But the problem is that when booking a flight, sometimes all the seats you like are already taken.

The **Seat Alerts** app is available for both Android and iPhone users, and it was developed precisely to help you get your favorite seat. It allows you to create an alert that lets you know when your favorite seat (window seat in my case) becomes available.

When you receive the alert, you just have to call the airline quickly and request to change your seat, especially if you like the window seat. Because if we're on the same flight, there will be at least two of us wanting to sit there.

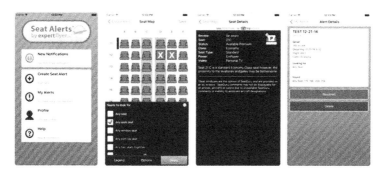

Visit: https://www.expertflyer.com/free-program.

Keeping Track of Flights

Obviously, the best-case scenario is that your flight arrives on time and at the correct gate. But we all know that in most cases, this just doesn't happen.

Secret 33: FlightAware

To help you keep track of any delays and changes that may happen to your flight, I recommend the **FlightAware** app. It allows you to track flights online, see a live map of the flight moving, and keep track of any delays, cancellations, and gate changes. This app is available for both Android and iPhone smartphones.

And the web-based version is also great:

Visit: https://flightaware.com/.

Secret 34: FlightStats

With **FlightStats**, you can track flights almost anywhere in the world. You just need a specific flight number, route, or airport. After your search, the information will be saved in the My Flights tab so you can access it easily later.

The best feature this app offers is the real-time flight-tracker live map, where you can see the exact position of the aircraft. What's more, you can choose from several different settings to include the flight plan, route, weather radar, and so on. You can also easily share the flight info directly from the app.

Visit: https://www.flightstats.com.

Secret 35: Flightradar24

In this app, you can select a flight to see more info about the route, estimated arrival time, speed, altitude, and more. Of course, you can also look for a specific flight by flight number, airline, or airport. Once you select a specific airport, you will get more information, such as current weather conditions and delay stats.

However, what sets this app apart from the rest is that you can check what flights are currently over your head just by pointing your device at the sky. The phone uses its camera to spot the aircraft so you can learn everything about the flight and even get to see what the pilot sees in 3D. For me, this is just awesome.

Visit: https://www.flightradar24.com/.

Part 4: Saving on Car Rentals

Car rental companies are greedy. Not as greedy as airlines companies, but they can sometimes really get on your nerves. But hey, this book wouldn't be THE BOOK about travel if it didn't include useful tips for renting a car, right?

Classic Car Rental Companies

You're old school, and you like renting a car the old-fashioned way – with companies such as Hertz, Avis, and Sixt. No problem, there are many ways to save when renting a car at these companies.

Secret 36: Rental Car Reward Programs

Just like airlines, car rental companies also offer membership programs. They are easy to sign up for and are usually free as well.

Some of the advantages of these programs are free upgrades and the ability to skip the lines. Also, most companies will save your car-rental preferences, guarantee vehicle availability for short-notice reservations, and give you rewards points that can be redeemed for free rentals or upgrades.

Here are some of the best car rental rewards programs that I believe are worth applying to:

- National Emerald Club

- Hertz Gold Plus

- Alamo Insiders

- Avis Preferred

- Budget Business Program

- Dollar Express Renter Rewards

- Enterprise Plus

- Thrifty Blue Chip Rewards

Secret 37: Kayak (Again)

Remember our good old friend Kayak? Well, it does a lot more than just search for the best flight deals. It can also search for the best car rental deals for you.

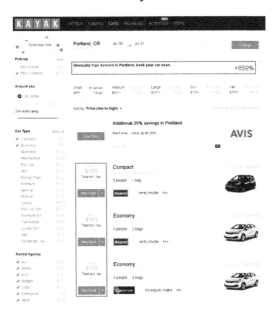

Just like it does for flights, it gives you many customization options for your search, compares its offers to other search websites, and overall, it's the best option for searching for car rental deals.

Secret 38: Prepay Is the Best Pay

When booking a car rental online, you are usually given two options: prepay online or pay when picking up the car.

Your best option is to prepay because that way, you'll save money. Usually, the price difference is as much as 20 percent when prepaying for your rental car. Those savings add up even more during longer rentals.

Next time when you're booking a car rental, be smart and prepay for it, so you keep your money in your pockets and out of the rental company's pockets.

Secret 39: Avoid Renting a car at the Airport

Sometimes, when taking a last-minute flight, you just don't have enough time to book your car rental in advance. In that case, getting your car from one of the car rental companies at the airport may seem like the best idea. However, doing so is a huge mistake, since renting a car at the airport usually costs 10 to 30 percent more than what you would pay at another location.

Instead, just take a cab to another location where you can rent a car and avoid the airport option altogether. Doing so will take a little more of your time, and it certainly isn't ideal when you have some urgent business to take care of. However, it will definitely save some of your hard-earned money.

Secret 40: Use Your Membership

Don't be shy about asking your rental company for a discount. You may be surprised by what you get. Many car rental companies offer military discounts, AAA membership discounts, senior discounts, corporate discounts, and many others.

Secret 41: Thanks, but No Thanks

Rental companies offer a bunch of additional stuff so they can get you to pay more, such as extra insurance and prepaid gas. The extra insurance is really unnecessary if you already have your own car insurance or an AAA membership. Also, there are some credit cards that offer free car rental insurance, so make sure you know all the benefits of your credit card.

The prepaid gas offered by rental companies is almost always more expensive than just filling the tank up at a nearby gas station. However, don't fill the car up just before delivering it back because gas stations near car rental companies are usually more expensive.

Secret 42: Sneaky Fees

Finally, there are sneaky fees that rental car companies adore. Here is how to avoid them easily.

If you're not prepaying for the gas, check the amount of gas you have in your tank before you drive off. If it's not at the same level when you return it, you'll be charged an extra fee.

Also make sure to check the car for any damage both on the outside and the inside, and don't hesitate to take some photos or even video. You should do this both before driving off and when returning the car. This way, you're covered in case the rental company tries to charge you for any damage that was not your fault.

Sometimes, when delayed, you just can't drive the car back on time. If that happens, call the rental company and check if it is cheaper just to extend the rental instead of paying late fees.

Lastly, avoid asking for additional items such as GPS and satellite radio. They come at an extra cost added to every day you rent the car and can add up when your credit card bill arrives at the end of the month. Besides, almost all smartphones provide accurate GPS navigation with up-to-date traffic alerts.

There are also a bunch of apps for your smartphone, such as Spotify, Apple Music, YouTube, and Pandora that give you a variety of choices for music. Just remember to bring your auxiliary cable or use Bluetooth to connect your phone to the car's sound system and a nice phone holder for the dashboard. I never leave without mine.

Modern Car Rentals

On the other hand, some people are more comfortable with modern car rental options. There are quite a few options out there, but Turo is the one I highly recommend.

Secret 43: Turo

Turo is an app available for Android and iPhone. A car rental company that works differently than most other companies, Turo has been around since 2010 and has thousands of cars across more than 5,500 cities around the world. It works as an intermediary between people who rent out their cars and those who want to rent a car.

The rental prices are determined by the individual car owners, while Turo takes a cut on the price. However, their prices are usually cheaper than those of traditional car rental companies.

There are three different options for insurance: premium, basic, or no protection. I recommend you choose premium because it comes with both personal liability as well as covering lost, stolen, or damaged costs. Premium coverage can cost as little as $9, while traditional rental companies charge around $40 for the same thing.

For all of you younger travelers out there, while almost all traditional car rental companies only allow you to rent a car if you're at least twenty-five, Turo allows you to rent a car if you're twenty-one or older.

Turo also shows reviews from users who have already rented a specific car before and lets you know the quality, condition, and cleanliness of the car beforehand. Picking up the car can be a lot more practical as well – just meet up with the car owner, and your adventure can start.

With Turo, you can save in two different ways. While it gives you a cheaper – and better – option for renting a car, it also gives you the chance to earn money when not using your car. All you have to do is rent it out while you're traveling.

Still, I wouldn't recommend Turo to people who plan on traveling long distances using a rented car. Very few owners offer one-way rentals because they just don't want to travel to a remote location. Also, they are not very fond of you adding thousands of miles to their car.

Overall, though, I consider Turo a superior option to conventional car rentals – the best, cheapest, and most practical way of renting a car.

I've used it many times to find those hard-to-get minivans when traveling with the kids, and it's been a true game changer. We once rented from someone at Dallas Love Field, and he delivered the car to the airport door, right outside the baggage claim, so I didn't have to haul all my kids, bags, and car seats all the way to the shuttle and then the car rental location. He was waiting for me right outside the door, and it took us five minutes to be on our way. That's a big score in my book!

Visit: https://turo.com/.

Secret 44: Getaround

Getaround offers all types of cars for hourly and daily rentals with included insurance. As soon as you've paid for the rental, you can unlock their cars with your phone and drive off.

With Getaround, you can rent cars, trucks, and even vans. Finally, all Getaround trips are covered with insurance and 24/7 roadside assistance.

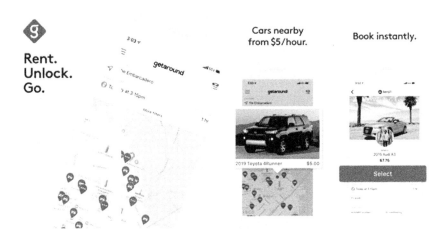

Visit: https://www.getaround.com/.

Part 5: Getting a Ride Safely

Maybe you don't want to drive a car while traveling after all. You may not be a big fan of driving, or you just want to relax knowing that somebody can take you where you need to be.

But we all know how traditional taxi services can often overcharge, not provide a good experience during the ride, and if they really want to screw you over, choose longer routes so they can charge you more.

No worries, there are several options out there for you that beat the traditional taxi services. All of the following services/apps are offered both for iPhone and Android.

Secret 45: Curb (US)

If you are located in the United States and still want to use licensed taxis to get around the city but with a modern touch, you should definitely consider Curb. The service is available in more than sixty US cities and will only call on licensed taxi drivers to get you where you need to go.

You can make payments through the app using cash or other payment methods, such as a credit card, if the taxi has a credit card reader. The app also allows you to schedule rides up to twenty-four hours in advance.

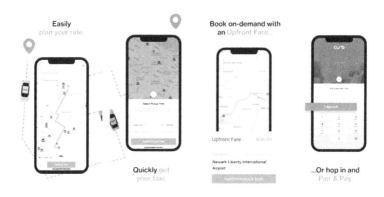

Visit: https://gocurb.com/.

Secret 46: Cabify by Easy Taxi (Worldwide)

Cabify uses the same principle as Curb – licensed taxis and modern payment methods. The main difference is that Cabify (Easy Taxi) operates in thirty countries worldwide, and it has become one of the most popular apps of its kind. Although it started in Brazil, Easy Taxi has expanded beyond South and Central America to include cities in Africa, the Middle East, and Asia.

Visit: http://www.easytaxi.com.

Secret 47: Uber (US/Europe)

Who hasn't heard about Uber? I'd say even my ninety-six-year-old grandfather has heard of it! Uber is the absolute most popular ridesharing app, the one that pioneered this type of service. It works in most parts of the world and accepts all major payment cards.

Their drivers go through serious background checks to prove they can drive people around safely. They also have to present documentation to Uber, such as a driver's license, in order to prove they are competent and reliable drivers.

After each ride, the driver receives a rating of one to five stars and also rates his passenger in the same way. Drivers who fail to provide good service and have their rating drop below a certain level are banned from driving with Uber. Also, passengers who are polite and maintain a high passenger score are usually able to get some of the highest-rated drivers in their vicinity.

On top of that, Uber offers some of the cheapest prices on the market as well as reward points for people who use their services often. The rewards can be used for free rides, priority pick-up at the airport, and priority customer service.

Of all the services on this list, Uber is the one I use and recommend the most. They offer the highest-quality service available, great prices, and good customer support and have a worldwide presence. I have used their service for years now, and

I can honestly tell you that there only have been a couple of times that I didn't have a great experience with Uber.

Visit: https://www.uber.com/.

Secret 48: Lyft (US)

Lyft was created around the same time as Uber, and it is Uber's best-known competitor. It has similar prices to Uber and a similar rating system for drivers, though it also has a fair share of downsides.

Lyft has fewer drivers than Uber, a different reward program, and the app isn't as easy to use as Uber. My personal experience has also taught me that a lot of Lyft cars aren't as good (or new) as the ones used by Uber drivers.

But if you don't like Uber as a company for whatever reason, then Lyft is a decent alternative. They generally aren't as good as Uber, but they will definitely get the job done and provide a good experience for a similar price.

Visit: https://www.lyft.com/.

Secret 49: Careem (Africa/Middle East)

Another ridesharing app similar to Uber, **Careem** operates in cities across Northern Africa and the Middle East. They offer multiple levels of service, a reward system, and the option to book in advance.

If you find yourself in the region where Careem operates and can't find an Uber, Careem is a solid choice to get you where you need to go – safely and at a fair price.

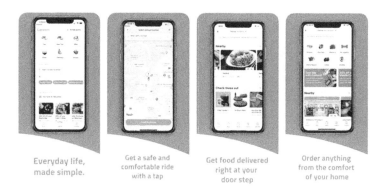

Visit: https://www.careem.com.

Secret 50: Didi Chuxing (China)

This is the Chinese version of Uber, which operates in hundreds of cities in China and has millions of drivers. Besides hailing their own cars, they also offer you the option to set up a carpool or even hire a designated driver.

Didi Chuxing has been so outstanding at providing its services that it was able to win a long and fierce war with the actual Uber company for dominance in China – so much so that Uber finally decided to sell its China division to Didi Chuxing. If you're in China, Didi Chuxing is obviously the best choice for a ridesharing service.

Visit: https://www.didiglobal.com/.

Secret 51: Grab (Asia)

Grab operates in Southeast Asia, in locations such as Indonesia, Malaysia, the Philippines, Singapore, Thailand, and Vietnam. They have 75,000 drivers and a user base of almost four million people.

They offer several different types of transportation. Their Grab app is used to hail licensed taxis, their GrabCar app offers a ridesharing service similar to Uber, and their GrabBike app offers motorcycles instead of cars.

If you're in a hurry, GrabBike can be pretty useful to avoid the infamous heavy traffic in the region. If you're in this region, Grab will live up to your expectations, providing the best service for the price and getting you where you need to go.

Visit: https://www.grab.com/.

Secret 52: Ola (India)

Ola is India's largest ridesharing service, offering many different types of transportation, like luxury car rides, Uber-like services, licensed taxis, and even rickshaw rides.

If you need a specialized service in India that Uber doesn't provide, like a rickshaw ride, for example, Ola could be a useful alternative.

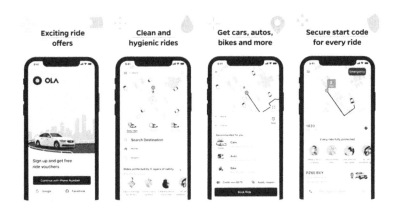

Visit: https://www.olacabs.com/.

Secret 53: BlaBlaCar

With BlaBlaCar, you can share rides with local drivers by pitching in for gas.

You just need to request a seat, the driver has to approve, and that's it. There is no doubt that this is both a cheap and interesting way to get from point A to point B. Plus, it beats buses and trains easily.

Visit: https://www.blablacar.com/.

Secret 54: GasBuddy

Why is this app awesome? Because it can find you the best gas prices in the US and Canada. You will never have to pay full price at the gas station again. Instead, you can save money by always knowing what station has the cheapest gas.

To make things even better, you can earn free gas automatically. This company has partnered up with some of the retailers you already shop at, so all your purchases count toward getting affordable or free gas.

Visit: https://www.gasbuddy.com/.

Secret 55: Gumtree

Gumtree is the Craigslist for globetrotters. Travelers use this website to find travel buddies, share rides, or even get employed. With Gumtree, a traveler can find second-hand gear, homestays, and other things that can come in handy when traveling.

Visit: https://www.gumtree.com/.

Part 6: Public Transportation Secrets

Either by preference or financial necessity, some people have to use public transportation when traveling. But this isn't necessarily a bad thing, as it can help you get immersed in the culture you are visiting big time. Moreover, there are apps that can help you with this.

Secret 56: TripGo

The most advanced public transportation app is **TripGo**. It works on Android and iPhone, offering a variety of features. It lets you compare and combine any transportation methods, such as trains, buses, taxis, subways, metros, cabs, trams, your own or shared car or bike, motorcycle, or ride-share.

TripGo provides real-time information about public transport and makes it easy to compare the prices between different options. It can also sync with your calendar so you can time your transportation correctly and not miss any important activities. The fact that the app has received seven awards since 2012 is enough proof of how reliable it is.

However, its biggest weakness is not being available in more places. Don't get me wrong, it's available in a lot of places, but for the most part, they're major cities. I recommend you check online if it supports the location where you plan to use public transport, before fully relying on it.

Visit: https://tripgo.com/.

Secret 57: Transit

The **Transit** app doesn't have as many features as TripGo, but it has its strengths. Besides being reliable and easy to use, the Transit app works in more than 175 cities worldwide, which makes it a perfect alternative for people traveling to a location where TripGo doesn't work.

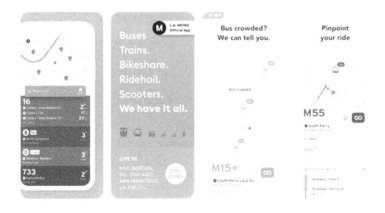

Visit: https://transitapp.com/.

Secret 58: Citymapper

One of the best public transport apps out there, Citymapper is great for travelers, especially if you're lost. Just open the app and tap the nearby bus stop on the map, and you will see information about the lines, such as the arrival time and how to get to your destination. This app also lets you compare your trip options by time and cost, which is really useful.

Visit: https://citymapper.com.

Secret 59: Moovit

Moovit is another awesome public transport app but simpler than Citymapper, for example. It is divided into three categories: directions, stations, and lines.

With it, you can route your trip or search for real-time arrival info at any bus stop or train station. The best thing about this app is that it works in over two thousand cities around the world.

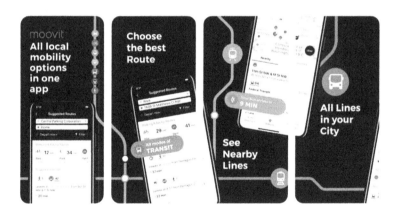

Visit: https://moovitapp.com/.

Secret 60: Rail Europe

This company is a worldwide distributor of European rail services, so it will most definitely come in handy if you're planning to travel through Europe by train.

With Rail Europe, you can get railway passes, train tickets, and reservations. As a matter of fact, many travelers claim that

Rail Europe has saved them hundreds of bucks on their journeys through Europe, thanks to its great rail pass deals.

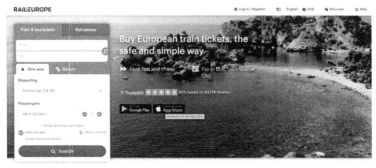

Discover Europe by train

Visit: https://www.raileurope-world.com/.

Secret 61: The Man in Seat Sixty-One

The Man in Seat Sixty-One is a website that serves as the ultimate guide for train travel all around the globe. The website has the most comprehensive information on routes, times, prices, and train conditions.

All in all, with The Man in Seat Sixty-One, you'll no longer have to deal with dilapidated trains and bad routes.

Visit: https://www.seat61.com/.

Part 7: Accommodation Secrets

You arrived at your destination, you know how to get to the most famous landmarks in the city, but you have a strange feeling that you forgot something really important . . . like finding a place to stay.

Joking aside, accommodation is definitely something you should take care of way before you actually get on a plane. Either way, here are my recommendations for places to stay while traveling.

Searching for & Booking a Hotel

Depending on your budget, a hotel can be relatively modest, with a decent breakfast, or it can be extremely luxurious with huge, delicious meals and extras such as a pool, sauna, and spa. But what all hotels have in common is a cleaning staff who prepares your room beforehand and also cleans it during your stay, as well as replaces towels and bedsheets, which can be pretty useful.

I absolutely love staying in 4- or 5-star hotels. In fact, I stay in hotels 99 percent of the time whenever I travel.

If you love hotels as much as I do, here are some useful resources to find the best deals.

Secret 62: Kayak (One Last Time, I Promise)

Yes, I'm recommending Kayak again. The thing with Kayak is that it's a real giant in the travel industry and very efficient at finding you the best hotel deals currently available as well as helping you choose a hotel that suits your needs.

Kayak offers you a variety of different ways to customize your hotel searches, such as selecting only hotels with a certain number of stars or only hotels near a certain zip code. It also compares its deals to other booking websites so you can be sure you're getting the best deal possible.

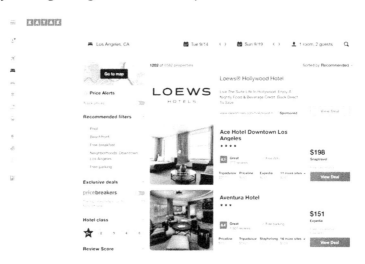

Secret 63: Verifying with TripAdvisor

When I find a hotel that looks great and is within my price range, but I'm not 100 percent sure if it's a good choice, I turn to TripAdvisor. It has an enormous database of hotels and restaurants all around the world with real reviews from real people. In fact, that's the main reason it's the best tool for figuring out if a hotel is really as good as it seems to be.

On TripAdvisor, you can find non-Photoshopped pictures and description of the hotel and its rooms, information about its location, and most useful of all, honest reviews by people who have already stayed there. TripAdvisor is definitely the most respected and recommended hotel review website and also has my recommendation. It is necessary to use it when you want to make sure you're booking the right hotel.

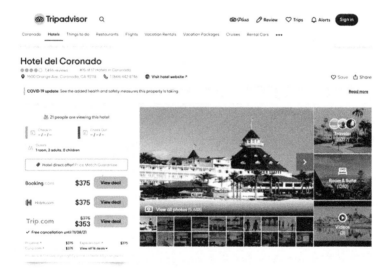

Visit: https://www.tripadvisor.com/.

Secret 64: Four-Star Hotels For the Price of Two-Star?

Sounds too good to be true? Just wait.

Hotwire is a website that offers discounted prices that sometimes go unbelievably low. It uses its relationships with some of the leaders in the travel industry, helping them sell hotel rooms, airline seats, and rental cars that they otherwise wouldn't be able to sell.

That way, Hotwire offers deals at much lower prices than other websites. And all of that without any bidding or guessing on the customer's side.

Visit: https://www.hotwire.com/.

Secret 65: Roomer

Basically, when people can't go on a trip and cancel their reservation at the last minute, hotels put these rooms on Roomer, where they sell them at a discount to get some of the money back.

Honestly, I've never used this website, so I'm not telling you this from my experience, but I've heard decent things about it from my friends. It's definitely worth a try.

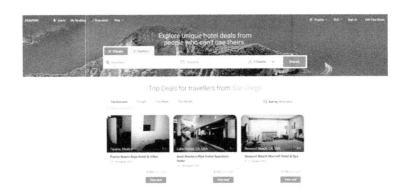

Visit: https://www.roomertravel.com.

Secret 66: Agoda (Asia)

Agoda is a hotel booking service for hotels and guesthouses in Asia. It lets you sort search results to find the lowest price or the highest-rated hotels for your target dates. It also offers secret deals that are selected for you by the app. These are usually at discounted rates, sometimes as much as 80 percent off!

You can filter your results, select your price range and amenities, and remove or add certain types of accommodations. Overall, Agoda is a good place to start if you're looking for great deals in Asia.

Visit: https://www.agoda.com.

Secret 67: Uncovering Last-Minute Deals from Top-Rated Hotels

If you're looking for cheap last-minute deals for hotels, HotelTonight is at your service.

Similar to Hotwire, this website has a network of high-quality hotels around the world, and it works as a middleman between the hotels and the customers. When a hotel needs to fill rooms for the night, it offers them as a last-minute deal on HotelTonight, which lets you save up to 70 percent on hotel rooms.

For example, one time I found a crazy-hot deal on this website, which was $150 cheaper than on Booking.com. And only because I booked it for the same night.

Visit: https://www.hoteltonight.com/.

Secret 68: Name Your Price . . .

One of the oldest hotel-booking websites, Priceline allows you not only to get hotel rooms but also flights, cruises, and car rentals. One of the biggest benefits of this site is that you can book all of this at once, saving yourself a bunch of money.

Generally, you can expect to save anywhere from 18 to 40 percent on their deals, but don't be surprised if you discover huge discounts – even up to 60 percent.

One of the best things about Priceline is that you can name your own price by selecting the general location, set the price you're willing to pay, enter your information, and wait for the offer to arrive.

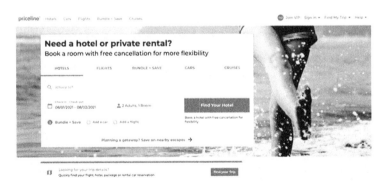

Visit: https://www.priceline.com/.

Secret 69: Lower Prices at Business Hotels

Sometimes business hotels can give you amazing deals, and this is especially true if you are traveling in Europe. You see, the thing with business hotels is that they usually have fewer guests on weekends and in the summer. So to get more guests into their rooms, they lower their prices at those times.

Secret 70: Booking a Hotel with No Down Payment

Booking.com may be the most popular site where people find accommodation. It offers a huge choice of cheap hotels, hostels, and other types of accommodation.

One thing I personally like about Booking.com is that it's fast and easy, and it has a no-money-down policy. That means if I have to cancel my reservation or change my travel dates, I don't have to pay a penalty.

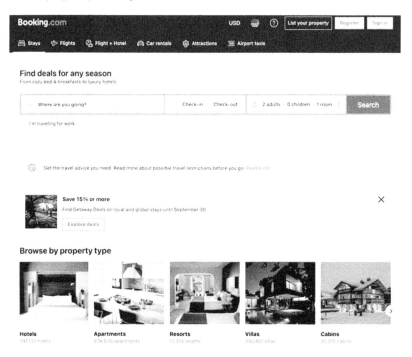

Visit: https://www.booking.com.

Secret 71: The Rate Parity Rule and How to Beat It

Accommodations are undoubtedly one of the top-two largest expenses involved in travel, and they are one of the most important factors for an enjoyable stay.

However, it is very hard to find deeply discounted rates on a nice hotel. One of the main reasons for this is a tricky little phrase: *rate parity*.

Rate parity is a legal agreement put in place between online travel agencies (OTAs) and hotels that ensures neither business is undercutting the other on price. In theory, it makes sense; an online booking site and hotel agree to publish the same nightly rate to the public, giving neither an unfair advantage in getting your business. But in practice, it disables the hotel's ability to offer you a proper discounted rate. If they drop the rate on their personal website, for example, that rate would have to drop for OTAs as well, creating an endless cycle where savings never actually get passed on to the public.

So how do you beat it? Easy!

Find a reliable, trustworthy, members-only travel club like TheTravelSecret!

This works because the rate parity rule doesn't apply to closed-platform travel businesses like TheTravelSecret – or the clients they serve. These services, including time-shares and other travel membership clubs that work directly with clients, can negotiate around common roadblocks like rate parity.

For example, take TheTravelSecret's listed rates for a popular resort and spa in Los Cabos, Mexico. On all well-known OTAs, the public price for a stay in the 4.5-star accommodation is upward of $5,000, and even over $7,000 for one listing.

Meanwhile, TheTravelSecret members' privately-listed price is just $1,850 for the same room on the exact same dates – a 67 percent discount, a savings of almost $4,000. This is for the same top-notch accommodations in a prime location.

The benefits of such services also extend to things like cruises, rewards that help travelers save on flights, car rentals, tours, and visiting popular tourist attractions. If you want to travel often, they are a great way to save money.

Visit: https://www.thetravelsecret.com.

Secret 72: Rocketmiles: Book & Earn

This is one of my favorites.

A part of Booking Holdings, which is the leader in the global travel industry, Rocketmiles can help you find hundreds of thousands of accommodations in all parts of the world. You can also use it to earn rewards and then use those rewards to make another trip with loyalty miles.

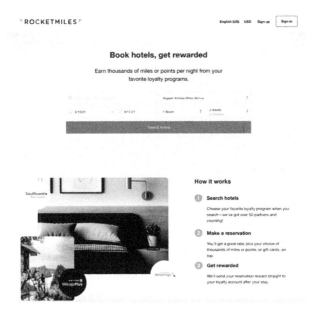

Visit: https://www.rocketmiles.com/.

Secret 73: Hotel Loyalty Programs

Just like with free flights, you can also get free hotel stays by collecting points and using loyalty programs.

The best way to do this is to stay at hotels that are part of the loyalty programs you're a member of.

Some of the best hotel loyalty programs out there are:

- GHA Discovery

- Leaders Club

- Ritz Carlton Rewards

- Expedia Rewards

- Trump Card

- Sirius by Jumeirah

- World of Hyatt

- Marriott Bonvoy

- Le Club AccorHotels

- Hilton Honors

- Golden Circle by Shangri-La

- IHG Rewards Club

If you're not yet a part of any loyalty programs, make sure to find out which loyalty programs your favorite hotels participate in and start your membership with them.

Another very popular way to collect hotel membership points, just like with the airline programs, is to use your credit card to earn points and then transfer those points to the hotel program. Eventually, when you have enough points, you'll be able to book a hotel room for free. Some people use this system so efficiently that when they travel, they get both their plane tickets and hotel rooms for free. Definitely something to bear in mind.

Secret 74: Reciprocal Benefits

Some of the major hotel chains and airlines form partnerships to give their customers better deals. For example, American Airlines and Hyatt Hotels are planning on providing frequent travelers additional ways to earn miles, points, and status every time they fly with American or stay at Hyatt.

This way, you can use loyalty programs to get rewards and earn more points and miles, combining them and booking a dream holiday.

You can read about reciprocal programs on each program's website. This way, you are up to date with the latest details.

Secret 75: Book a Room at a New Property

If you're a fan of new hotels and fresh places, check out Newsleeps – a website that offers new places for people to stay. They gather data about the hotels that are about to open, as well as those that have been recently opened or renovated.

HINT: Most of the time, new hotels offer super-cheap deals as part of their grand opening celebration. ;-)

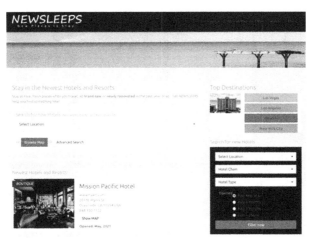

Visit: https://www.newsleeps.com.

Secret 76: Same Room, Cheaper Price

Pruvo is a great tool for saving money *after* booking a hotel.

Let's say you found the right hotel, booked it at the best available price, and now you're done, right? Not really. There is a website called Pruvo that can still help you.

After creating your account with Pruvo, send them your hotel reservation information. If there are any better deals than the one you got, Pruvo will let you know. That way, you can book the exact same room for a better price than you originally paid.

However, it is important to note that when making your hotel reservation, there has to be a free cancelation policy for Pruvo to work. If your hotel reservation can't be canceled without any fees or can't be canceled at all, then Pruvo is not a good option.

Visit: https://www.pruvo.net/.

Secret 77: Price Alerts

If you want to get a chance to hunt down the best deals, you may want to take advantage of price alerts. One of the ways to do this is by signing up for email alerts on one of the hotel booking websites I've mentioned.

I know this option definitely works on Kayak. All you have to do is log into your free Kayak account and click Emails + Alerts in the drop-down menu in the top right corner. When you see the hotel alerts option, set your maximum price for your destination and wait for the email to arrive.

How about a Gift Card?

Did you know that you can book major hotel chains with hotel gift cards? For instance, check out the website Gift Card Granny for discounted gift cards, and use them to book your hotel. In a nutshell, you can use this website to find some of the best gift cards around, including the ones for hotels.

Best of all, gift card purchases also count toward point earnings and traveler status.

Visit: https://www.giftcardgranny.com/.

Use Discounts

If you are part of the AARP or AAA, you can get special rates which are much more affordable than regular ones. Fun fact: anyone can join the AARP. I'm a member too. They have amazing travel benefits (including deals on hotels and British Airways flights). It's well worth the membership.

Why Don't You Just Call Them?

Want a better deal? Call up a hotel and ask for one. If you want to get things at lower prices, sometimes you just have to bargain.

It's very simple. Just call the hotel and ask for a discount. Sometimes they can give you better rates, especially if it's during midweek at some nonpeak time of year.

Bonus Tip: Check the Location of Your Hotel

Generally, if your accommodation is farther away from the center of the city, it will very likely come at a cheaper price. However, this also means that you will need more time and even money when going downtown.

Make sure not to book a room on the outskirts of the city, but rather find a compromise between price and location.

Secret 78: Rent a Property

Your next option is to rent a property during your travel. This can give you more privacy than a hotel, more space, and in most cases, a working kitchen as well.

There are a handful of apps that enable you to rent a property while you're traveling, but something tells me you already know which one is the best.

Airbnb

Airbnb is both a website and an app, and the app is available for both Android and iPhone. It gives you a wide selection of properties around the world to choose from, such as apartments, condos, and houses to rent. You can also filter your search to include only properties with certain amenities, such as a pool or jacuzzi.

The owners/hosts receive reviews from the people who stay at their properties, which means you can rest easy when booking a place to stay. If a host has bad reviews, you'll be able to see it easily and exclude them from your list.

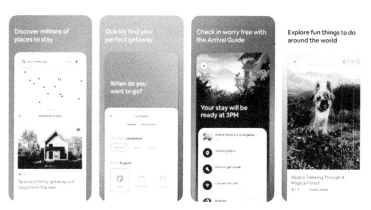

Visit: https://www.airbnb.com/.

Depending on how much you're planning to spend on your rental and if you're booking at least fourteen days in advance, you can pay just half of the rental when booking and the rest before checking out. This is helpful for people who can't afford or simply don't want to make one lump sum payment at the time of booking.

Overall, I highly recommend Airbnb. It is popular worldwide, has been around for years, and makes renting a place easy and simple. Definitely an option to consider for people who want something cozier than a hotel.

Secret 79: Stay in a Home Exchange

Home exchange programs have been around for quite some time now, and that's why they are really popular among older generations. However, nowadays a lot of youngsters are trying this option as well.

So, what is a home exchange? For a set amount of time, you swap homes with a family from another country. Of course, a lot of people are not really fond of this option, since they are worried about security. However, bear in mind that the other family trusts you with their home too.

So before you actually exchange your home with someone else, get to know the family, talk with them, see if it can work, and only then make a decision.

Top websites that offer home exchange opportunities are:

- https://Homeexchange.com

- http://Ihen.com

Secret 80: Hostel

If you need a budget-friendly accommodation, something cheaper than a hotel, then a hostel may be just what you need.

But what is your first association when you think of a hostel? A room with fifteen beds and not being able to sleep because that guy is snoring so damn loud? Well, I have to tell you one thing – that's a thing of the past. Nowadays, most hostels offer smaller, even double rooms where you can have a lot of privacy.

There is quite a lot of prejudice when it comes to hostels. A lot of people consider them to be appropriate just for young people or think they are dirty and scary places. But that couldn't be further from the truth.

In fact, many adults stay in hostels as well. Also, most modern hostels come with Wi-Fi, tour desks, bars, curtains, lockers for your stuff, big bathrooms, and more. They are also constantly improving and getting better every year.

And while it's true that there are hostels intended specifically for younger guests, international hostel chains such as Hostelling International focus on better service and group travelers.

Overall, hostels are not only safe but also one of the best-value options out there. They're great for people of all ages, and you really don't have to be an adventure-seeking backpacker to stay in one. So forget about the silly horror movies and consider booking a hostel, especially if you're tight on budget.

In this case, I am not recommending Kayak for booking your stay. The best option for booking a hostel is the website and app called Hostelworld. It will show you the best deals available and let you choose from a wide selection of hostels around the world.

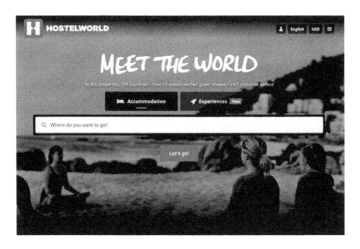

Visit: https://www.hostelworld.com/.

Secret 81: Crashing at Someone's Place

Have you ever felt lonely while traveling or really wanted to get to know the culture of the place you were visiting? Was there a time when you wanted to travel but had no money to pay for accommodation? If yes, Couchsurfing is the solution.

Couchsurfing is a website and app available for iPhone and Android smartphones which allows you to stay at someone's home for free. It has a massive community of people across the globe and is widely regarded as the leader in this type of service.

If you're worried about your safety when staying at a stranger's home, you can relax. Similar to Airbnb, Couchsurfing allows you to leave reviews on both hosts' and guests' profiles. Also, every person using the app has to have a photo of themselves and have their profile filled out. What's more, Couchsurfing offers different levels of verification in order to guarantee safety.

I understand if you feel anxious. In fact, I felt the same before trying Couchsurfing, and I expect that is a pretty normal feeling the first time using it. But keep in mind one thing – a lot of the hosts who are part of the community are also travelers who want to help other travelers feel great staying at their place.

Visit: https://www.couchsurfing.com/.

Besides the strong community, a great thing about Couchsurfing is that you're able to meet and live with locals and really immerse yourself in their culture.

If you decide to give it a try, I recommend you carefully go through different profiles and pay attention to whether they are verified or not.

Here are also some similar websites you should check out:

- Global Freeloaders

- Hospitality Club

- Stay4free

Part 8: Where to Eat

For me, trying local food is one of the most important parts of traveling. Usually, I'm not a big eater, but when I'm in a foreign country, I want to try all kinds of new dishes, and I'm not ashamed to admit that I overeat every now and then. But it's worth it. Every time.

Of course, I don't recommend that you overeat, but trying new dishes definitely opens your mind, and if you're a gourmet, you'll probably want to add them to your collection. Here are some tips to improve the food experience wherever you go.

Secret 82: Feel Like Staying at the Hotel?

If you've had a long day and don't really feel like cooking or eating out, there's Uber Eats. It's more than obvious that the service is run by Uber, so you can rest assured that your experience will be top-notch.

Restaurants usually don't offer food delivery, but that's where Uber Eats comes in. This app shows you all the restaurants in the area that they work with, along with their menus, and allows you to order food.

You can order whatever you'd like to eat from the menu, and when the food is ready, an Uber driver will pick it up and deliver it straight to your door.

The service is usually pretty cheap, and sometimes Uber will even text you a promo code that gives you a couple of free deliveries. You can browse different restaurants based on the type of food they serve. Also, the restaurants have a star-based rating system, so you can try new ones without being afraid the food will be bad. Before ordering, you will get an estimate of how much time it will take for your food to arrive.

That means more convenience for you and less hassle whenever you're hungry but don't feel like leaving your hotel. Uber Eats definitely gets my recommendation for its practicality and ease of use – not only when traveling, but also in general.

Visit: https://www.ubereats.com.

Secret 83: Not Taking Any Chances

For people who don't mind leaving their hotel to get something to eat but aren't sure what restaurant to go to, OpenTable is your go-to app.

OpenTable shows you the restaurants near you, photos of them, and the different menu options. Best of all, you can make a reservation using the app. You're also able to share a restaurant with friends and family and pay the bill using the app in some restaurants.

Bottom line, OpenTable works worldwide and simplifies the process of choosing the restaurant you want to go to. It has definitely shown me amazing places and helped me avoid options with bad or overpriced food time and time again.

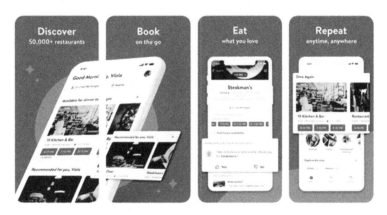

Visit: https://www.opentable.com/.

Secret 84: Use Pinterest

Though it may sound strange, Pinterest can be a very useful tool when looking for a solid restaurant. You can find pins from the locals, read their reviews, and even find the menu and prices so you know what to expect when you go there to grab a meal. Of course, the more pins and reviews a place has, the more likely it offers great service.

Visit: https://www.pinterest.com/.

Secret 85: Culinary Walking Tour

Have you ever gone on a culinary walking tour?

It includes a tour of the city's top-notch restaurants where you can try all the dishes they offer. Trust me on this one; it's quite an experience. And one thing is for sure – by the end of the walk, you'll definitely not be hungry anymore.

Secret 86: Eating with Good Company

Traveling without a companion can be a bit lonely sometimes, and that's all the more true when you're eating alone. Most people prefer having someone to talk to and having a couple of good laughs during their meals. The Eatwith app is a great solution if you're not a fan of eating alone, and it helps you get a better taste of the local culture at the same time.

The app connects you with hosts around the world that will prepare you food that's part of the local cuisine and keep you company during your meal. They offer experiences such as dinner parties, cooking classes, and much more. Eatwith is available in more than 130 countries, and it will help you have a fun experience during your travel.

Visit: https://www.eatwith.com/.

Part 9: Coming Home in One Piece

Having fun and extraordinary traveling experiences is what we all want out of our trips. But from time to time, we tend to forget how crucial it is to take all precautions in order to stay safe and get back home healthy and in one piece.

Secret 87: Staying Safe

We've all heard horror stories on the news – or even worse, from friends and family – about people being kidnapped, hurt, or killed while traveling. Even when going to safer destinations, it's always a good idea not only to be ready to act if anything bad happens but also to prevent dangerous situations in the first place. Here are some useful tips to help keep yourself safe when traveling.

Learn about Common Scams

Before you actually travel somewhere, do some research and find out if there are any scams typical of that place. This way, you will know what to expect and how to protect yourself.

Be wary of over-friendly locals that strike up a conversation as soon as they realize you're a foreigner. Also be extra careful when choosing discos and clubs when going out. You never know whether they will scam you with the prices or not.

Finally, find a reliable bank to exchange money. Some cities are known for money exchange scams and having different currency exchange rates for locals and foreigners. You can avoid this by going to a trusted bank or exchanging money before you even arrive.

Emergency Info

Should something go wrong, it's important that you know all the emergency numbers.

Getting mugged is bad enough, but having to walk around after that asking people for the police's number is even worse – not to mention if you need an ambulance.

That is why you should write down emergency info on a small card or a sheet of paper and carry it with you. This includes phone numbers of the police, ambulance, and your country's embassy.

It is also smart to upload copies of important documents to Dropbox or Google Drive that you can access them from anywhere in case you lose them.

Take Care of Your Valuables

Do not carry around things you can't afford to lose or have stolen. And if you can't avoid bringing some valuable items, you should keep them packed away and locked.

For example, there is a famous Bobby backpack that is really difficult to steal. Also, if you know that you're visiting a shady area of the city, wear your backpack on your front, not on your back.

Make sure to have number locks for your travel bags and lock them regularly. Also, phone your accommodation and see whether they offer a room safe or lockers of some kind. And carry the locker padlock with you – that is the surest way not to lose something you hold dear.

Keeping Your Passport Safe

Hackers and thieves are always coming up with new ways to steal your personal documents and identity, including your passport. And we all know that having your passport is extremely important.

If someone steals your identity – especially if you're in a foreign country – they can cause you a lot of problems, to say the least. I could list the potential problems for days, but one example would be using your identity to commit illegal activities. And if you know that some criminals can copy information from your passport without even stealing it, the situation gets even more alarming.

You know that modern passports have digital chips inside them. If a criminal gets close enough to you and your passport, they can read the information electronically stored on the chip without you ever knowing about it. So what can you do to avoid this?

That's where RFID-blocking passport holders come in. You can use them as regular passport holders, but they also block any scanners from reading your passport and stealing its information. They are relatively cheap to buy and easily can be found online on websites such as Amazon.

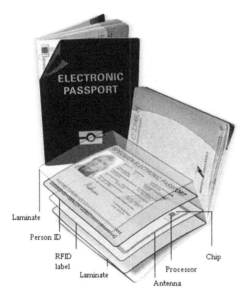

Knowing What's Going On

When traveling, it's important to know what's going on in the country or city you're visiting. The US State Department Smart Traveler app keeps you informed. True, it's the most useful to American citizens, but still very helpful to anyone who wants to know what's happening in the place they are traveling to.

The app frequently updates official information about the country, such as travel alerts, warnings, maps, and among other things, US embassy locations. It can be useful not only before your trip but while traveling as well. In case of a national emergency or some kind of attack, you'll always know what to do and where to go.

Visit: https://www.state.gov/.

Safe Running

Running is a part of the daily routine of many travelers, and it should remain that way when they go on a trip as well. The problem is that when you're in a foreign place, you don't know where it's safe to run. For example, some routes could be dangerous, with lurking muggers, or even worse. And that's one of the reasons why the MapMyRun app was created.

The app shows you the safest routes for you to run in cities worldwide. It shows you a selection of routes that are considered safe in the city where you are staying, gives maps of the chosen route, and then uses your phone's GPS to help you stay on it. The app is available for iPhone and Android.

Visit: https://www.mapmyrun.com/.

Secret 88: Staying Healthy

CDC

The American Center for Disease Control and Prevention (CDC) has a bunch of different apps, and the one that will be the most useful during your travels is their TravWell App.

When you open the app, you can find a checklist of what you need to do to prepare for your trip, destination-specific vaccine recommendations, and a customizable healthy-travel packing list.

Moreover, this app does the following:

- stores travel documents

- has a list of emergency services' phone numbers for every destination

- keeps a record of your medications and immunizations

- sets reminders to get vaccine booster doses or take any kind of necessary medication while you're traveling

Visit: https://www.cdc.gov/.

First Aid to the Rescue

Whether you're traveling or not, injuries are a part of life, so it's pretty useful to know what to do if you get injured. Fortunately, the American Red Cross created an app to help you in such situations.

The American Red Cross First Aid app is free and available in both English and Spanish. It shows you step-by-step guides on what to do in the case of allergies, bleeding, choking, broken bones, and other conditions. There are also tutorial videos that let you learn by watching others, as well as interactive quizzes to help you practice that knowledge yourself.

A friend told me about this app long ago when I started traveling often. Since then, the app has helped me a few times, and I can't recommend it enough.

Visit: https://www.redcross.org/.

Part 10: Saving on Your Phone Bill

Cell phone carriers have a special kind of passion for roaming for a very simple reason – it lets them charge you insane bills for using your phone overseas. And the worst part is that many people don't even need to pay all this extra money to stay connected. There are many other ways to keep using your phone while abroad that won't break the bank.

Secret 89: Local Carriers

Many local carriers offer affordable prepaid phone plans created exclusively for tourists. These plans usually come with a sufficient amount of internet data and calling minutes.

That means you can buy such a plan when you arrive at your destination, replace your old SIM card with the new one, and use the new number for as long as you stay in the new city. Voila! No pesky roaming fees from your home carrier!

However, when you buy a SIM card from one of the local carriers, remember to bring your passport, as many require an official foreign ID to give you the tourist phone plan. Why is this necessary? So locals don't take advantage of the cheap tourist phone plans.

Secret 90: WhatsApp

WhatsApp is an incredibly popular messaging app owned by Facebook. It is securely encrypted and allows you to send text and voice messages, pictures, videos, and documents, as well as make voice and video calls.

The service is widely considered to be very reliable, it's free, and it uses very little internet data. Adding someone is as simple as creating a contact for them with the number they have registered with the app, and that's it. WhatsApp will automatically recognize the number in your phone book and add that person to your WhatsApp contacts.

This app is ideal for travelers who don't have a lot of calling minutes available when roaming or in the case their tourist SIM card only offers internet data.

Visit: https://www.whatsapp.com.

One of the most popular alternatives to WhatsApp is Telegram. It practically offers the same features, so if you don't like WhatsApp for some reason, you can always use Telegram.

Visit: https://telegram.org/.

Secret 91: Google Fi

If you live in the United States, there is a solution that lets you continue using your regular number while traveling without breaking the bank. Believe it or not, Google has created a mobile phone carrier called Google Fi.

They offer an affordable monthly plan that provides a very reliable service. This is possible because they are partnered up with hundreds of different carriers and are allowed to use their cell towers.

They're very useful to people who travel, because they don't have any roaming charges for using your 4G data or texting, while they only charge twenty cents a minute for calling when you're out of the country.

Depending on how often you travel and how committed you are to your current provider, you should seriously consider trying Google Fi. Also, if you live outside the United States and really want to use the service, there are some very helpful guides online on how to do so.

Visit: https://fi.google.com.

Secret 92: Turn Off Cellular Data

Turning off cellular data is a must because if you fail to do it, roaming will be your worst enemy. Turning off your data will prevent you from unconsciously downloading huge updates and getting insane bills for it afterward. Also, it would be wise to turn off data roaming.

Secret 93: International Data Plan

Some people simply can't afford to be offline during their trips abroad if they work remotely, for example. And since you can't always find a Wi-Fi network to connect to, you should consider getting an international data plan.

Give your mobile carrier a call and ask about their international data plans. They will tell you what countries are available, how much each plan costs, and how you can activate the plan. Most companies can activate it for you, but some require you to activate it yourself from your phone.

For instance, T-Mobile provides free international data and text messaging. Calls are usually not free, but the pricing is extremely fair and affordable, so you won't have to worry about huge bills when you get back home.

Secret 94: Block Your Apps

When you're abroad and need to use data, it might come in handy to be able to control the data usage of certain apps on your phone. For instance, you can block apps from updating while you're traveling and thus avoid spending data on something that can definitely wait until you come back home.

Secret 95: Download Maps at Home

Before leaving home, download maps of the place you're visiting. While Google Maps can be used offline, you have to download the maps in order to access them later.

Apple Maps is a good option too, but many people claim Google Maps is better. If not sure which app to use, test out both apps and decide for yourself.

Part 11: Language Barriers

English is spoken all over the world, but sometimes you'll find yourself in a situation where you'll need to communicate with locals in their own language. Below I listed some apps that can help you find a common language with the local people everywhere you go.

Secret 96: Google Translate

Once again, Google comes to your rescue. This time, it's their Google Translate app. The app is free, it can translate more than one hundred languages, and many of them can be translated even when you're not connected to the internet.

However, bear in mind that, similar to Google Maps, offline translation requires you to download the specific language you want to translate before going offline.

Google wouldn't be Google if it didn't go above and beyond to satisfy its users. The app can also translate text from a picture, translate real-time voice conversations between two people, and even allow you to draw characters for translation that aren't available on a keyboard.

What's more, you can save your favorite translations or the ones you frequently use for future use. Translations easily be shared using social media, text messages, and other messaging apps.

Visit: https://translate.google.com/.

Secret 97: SayHi Translate

Google Translate is great at translating a bunch of different languages, but it sometimes struggles with idioms and local phrases. That's where the SayHi Translate app gets to shine, as it specializes in translating conversational and informal terms.

The app is available to both iPhone and Android users and is extremely useful to anyone who needs to translate informal conversations.

Visit: https://www.sayhitranslate.com/.

Secret 98: Duolingo

The Duolingo app teaches you how to write and speak a variety of languages correctly, giving you practice tasks that help you speak the language like a pro.

What makes it so special is that you only need to spend a small amount of time every day to learn the language you want. The app will remind you to practice, and you can configure the settings based on how fast you want to learn.

There are free and premium versions of the app, but for most travelers, the free version will be enough. This app is awesome because for just a little bit of your time and no money at all, you can learn several new languages.

Visit: https://www.duolingo.com/.

Part 12: Insurance

Obviously, none of us wants something bad to happen, but unfortunately, it sometimes does. And as much as we would like a first aid app to solve all the problems, sometimes you or someone you care about just needs to go to the hospital.

Or maybe it's just that your camera broke, your stuff was stolen, or you had an emergency that required you to go back home sooner than anticipated. In these cases, travel insurance can make a huge difference.

Travel insurance is an all-purpose emergency coverage that covers any of the above situations. It helps to protect you against various types of physical and financial harm, and although you may never have to use it, you'll be thankful you have it in case you do. However, bear in mind that there are certain situations that travel insurance doesn't cover, such as:

- injuries sustained while participating in extreme adventure activities
- emergencies caused by carelessness with your possessions
- emergencies caused by drug use
- pre-existing conditions

It is very important to know that travel insurance is not a replacement for your regular health insurance.

Also, you should buy the policy a few days before the trip because it usually takes twenty-four to forty-eight hours for it to activate. In other words, if you get injured before the policy becomes active, you won't be covered by it.

Secret 99: Look Beyond the Price

Of course buy the policy within your budget, but the price should not be the main factor when deciding what insurance you're going to get. Also bear in mind that the more you are prepared to pay, the lower your premium will be.

Secret 100: Annual Cover or Single-Trip

In general, there are two main types of travel insurance based on the length of your trip: single-trip and annual multi-trip. If you only go abroad once a year, single-trip insurance will do the trick. And it sometimes costs as little as a few bucks.

On the other hand, it is only logical that annual insurance is more expensive. But when you consider the fact that it covers everything whenever you leave your country, the price is very affordable.

Other things you should look out for:

- countries covered by the insurance

- maximum trip duration

- car insurance policy if you're planning to drive abroad

– baggage cover

– airline failure

Finally, make sure to buy a policy as soon as you book your trip. This way, you'll be able to use the insurance if your holiday gets canceled or delayed.

Secret 101: Family Insurance

When traveling with your partner and children, ask for family travel insurance. Also, always check with your insurer whether the policy covers your children if they happen to travel without you (e.g., school trips).

Secret 102: Medjet

Medjet offers premier international air medical transport and travel security membership programs. In other words, Medjet's got your back, and you can trust them to transfer you not only to the nearest acceptable medical facility, but also all the way back home to successfully recover.

This kind of insurance is awesome if you travel often, since you don't have to think about poor facilities or treatment, or even huge bills. You can even add travel security and crisis response to your policy.

Visit: https://medjetassist.com/.

Secret 103: World Nomads

World Nomads was created by an ex-nomad, which means they understand the mindset of a traveler and their needs. They have a great reputation, process claims quickly and easily, and offer great customer support. Also, their pricing is very affordable for the amount of protection their insurance provides.

They have even been endorsed by Lonely Planet and National Geographic for their quality of service. World Nomads has been my go-to choice for many years, and I can't recommend them enough.

We are World Nomads

Visit: https://www.worldnomads.com.

Part 13: Electronics and Internet

Now more than ever, electronics are an indispensable part of our lives. We carry around laptops, tablets, smartphones, smartwatches, and other electronics. And it seems that this is all the more true while traveling.

I want to share with you some cool tips and tricks you can put into action to get the most out of your electronics during your trip.

Secret 104: Check the Plug . . .

Different parts of the world use different types of power plugs. If you're traveling to a place that uses plugs which are incompatible with your chargers, then you need to buy a universal plug converter.

Try to avoid buying the adapter at the last minute, as airports and popular tourist locations at your destination will usually sell it at a much higher price. Instead, try buying it on Amazon or other similar websites where you can find good deals and read the reviews.

Secret 105: . . . And the Voltage

Most of North America, as well as some other countries, use 110-V electricity, while the rest of the world uses 220-V electricity. If you've traveled to different parts of the world, you know this can be a problem because some chargers work on both voltages, but others can't. If you plug a charger or any kind of electrical device that can only handle 110 volts into a 220-volt outlet, it will practically be fried and become useless.

That's why it's crucial to check all your electronics if you're traveling to a place with a different voltage. If some of them can't handle higher voltages, you can always use a universal voltage adapter like the one below.

Voltage adapters are harder to find than power plug adapters, so it's even more important to remember to buy them before the trip.

Secret 106: Best of Both Worlds?

If you're going to need both a power plug adapter and a voltage adapter, it would be foolish to buy them separately, because it will cost you more money. Instead, you should buy an adapter that takes care of both problems. One of the best adapters for both the plug type and the voltage is the Rapida Power Converter.

Secret 107: Power All Day

Running out of batteries can be extremely inconvenient, especially while traveling. Maybe you need your phone to listen to an audiobook while on a plane, or you need your laptop to finish a report. Whatever the reason, there is one perfect solution – a power bank.

A power bank is a battery that you can charge wherever you have an outlet nearby, pack it in your backpack, and then use it whenever you want to charge your electronics. There's a pretty wide range of power banks out there. Some can store more energy than others, but most of them can only charge your smartphone or tablet.

However, I recommend you buy Omni 20. It provides up to 100 watts of power and uses a high-quality 20,400 mAh battery. What does that mean? It's a very high-capacity battery that can power a lot of different stuff.

It doesn't just charge things like your laptop, smartphone, and tablet, but it can also power a device that doesn't use a battery, such as a TV or a projector. It's definitely more expensive than most other power banks, but it won't leave you high and dry when you need power. On the other hand, if you don't need as much power, Omni has other options with lower capacities, such as Omni 13.

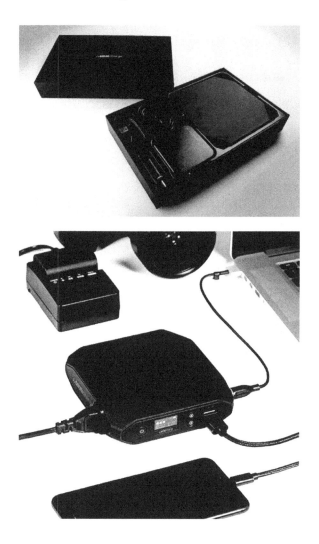

Secret 108: Wi-Fi Where?

If you've used up all your data or there's just no signal at a certain place, Wi-Fi is your only way to connect to the internet. But when you're traveling, you don't know where to connect to Wi-Fi or the password you need to use.

WiFi Map is a free app that comes in handy in such situations. It is basically a kind of social network where people share passwords for different Wi-Fi networks all around the world. They have more than one hundred million users and have shared more than 120 million different Wi-Fi hotspots so far. The app uses an interactive map to show Wi-Fi hotspots around you. Best of all, when you're online, you can also download all the Wi-Fi locations and passwords in the city to have offline access too.

Secret 109: Where Are My Photos?

Most people like taking photos to record the memories and experiences that happened during the trip. However, your phone can get stolen, or you could just drop it and break it. If that happens, you can always buy a new phone, but you can never take those pictures again. The good news is that you don't have to.

There are a number of apps that will automatically back up a photo on your phone to the cloud as soon as you take it. I recommend you go with Google Photos, which is a free and reliable app that uses your existing Google account to back up your photos automatically. That's not the best part of the app, though, as it gives you unlimited storage to back up your pictures for free.

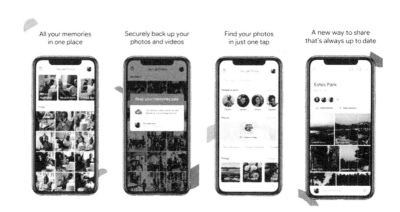

Visit: https://photos.google.com/.

Using Google Photos or another similar app will allow you to keep your travel memories safe and secure. Other similar apps that work well are Dropbox, Amazon Photos, and iCloud.

Part 14: Guides

Tour guides used to be the most popular choice when someone wanted to explore a new place. However, nowadays people are coming up with so many new ways that allow you to experience your destination from a completely different angle.

Below we listed both traditional and some modern ways you can use to discover all your destination has to offer.

Secret 110: Intrepid Travel

Intrepid started back in 1989, while two friends were traveling to Africa in a modified truck with no air conditioning. Darrell and Geoff filled the truck with supplies, beer, and aviator sunglasses, and then they realized that other people might like this type of travel too. Years later, Intrepid Travel is one of the most popular tour companies out there.

Intrepid Travel offers fantastic small group tours led by expert guides. Best of all, these tours leave a minimal environmental footprint, and you really get to meet a country along with its culture.

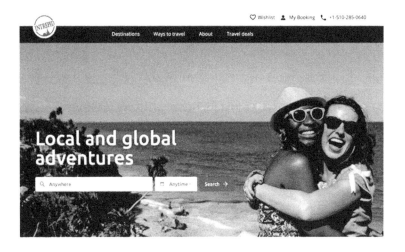

Visit: https://www.intrepidtravel.com/en.

Secret 111: Context Travel

Context is a leisure and travel company that organizes expert-led tours in the cultural capitals of the world, especially in Europe. They offer in-depth historic, food, and cultural tours.

What sets this company apart from the rest is the fact that it works as a network of people who are experts in travel themselves. For example, if you'd like to learn a thing or two about a country's cuisine, they will find a chef who will tell you all you need to know.

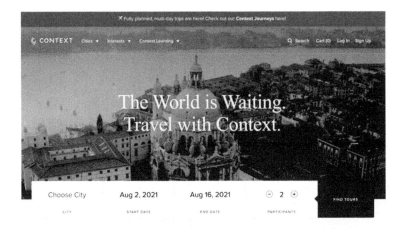

Visit: https://www.contexttravel.com/.

Secret 112: Showaround

Travelers around the globe are definitely changing the way they explore new places, and traditional tour guides are no longer as popular as they used to be.

Globetrotters are now seeking a more authentic experience, and they would rather spend some time with a local rather than with a professional guide. After all, who can better describe the place than a friendly local?

If you're looking for a local guide, a website called Showaround gathers the locals who are willing to show you their city. So instead of settling for the mainstream stuff, spend a day with a local and act like one. After all, isn't that the best way to meet a new city, culture, and people?

Visit: https://www.showaround.com/.

Secret 113: Guides by Lonely Planet

This app provides city guides that were expertly curated. You can fully rely on these guides, since the people who wrote them actually lived in each city they wrote about and experienced all the places and activities they recommended. Their guides include different recommendations, such as where to stay, what to do, and where to eat.

They have helped me discover amazing, off-the-beaten-track places that I would never have found on my own. The app also lets you save a city to view offline and bookmark your favorite cities. It also has ten thousand audio phrases for nineteen different languages in the case you need to speak to locals who don't speak English.

Visit: https://www.lonelyplanet.com/guides.

Secret 114: Sygic Travel

If you need a guide that can also help you organize your day, the Sygic Travel app is a great option. It is a free app (though it has a paid version too) that has guides for fifty million places, a 360-degree video option, and smart search filters. But what really sets this app apart is the way it helps you create a detailed itinerary to the minutest detail for each day of your trip.

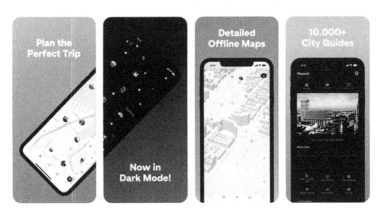

Visit: https://travel.sygic.com/en.

Part 15: Financials

Since very few people have an unlimited budget when they go on a trip, taking care of your personal finance is essential. Some apps can save you a lot of time and effort by helping you maintain your financials while away from home.

I can't emphasize enough how crucial it is to make copies of your bank account and credit card information, since this can save you a lot of stress while you're abroad. While this is a fundamental thing to do, you don't want to stop there.

Secret 115: Notify Your Bank about the Trip

You know that you can't use the money in your account when it's frozen. Since every deviation from your normal spending pattern – and we all know this regularly happens abroad – will raise a red flag for your bank, your account will get frozen and your credit card denied.

Luckily, you can avoid this by informing your bank and credit card companies about your trip.

Secret 116: Online Accounts

You should definitely set up an online bank account, since it can give you better control over your funds while you're abroad. With an online account, you can easily check your balances, transfer and deposit funds, and always be aware of all transactions.

Also, set up automatic payments, and you won't have to think about the bills when you are miles away from home.

Secret 117: Multiple Payment Methods

You should never rely on a single payment method. Instead, it's always good to have multiple options, such as cash, debit cards, and of course, credit cards.

Also, it would be great to have multiple bank accounts and credit cards, especially those that are accepted internationally.

Secret 118: No Foreign Transaction Fees

Signing up for the right travel rewards credit card will get you a wide range of benefits while traveling, such as no foreign transaction fees. This is great for all those who use credit cards as their main payment method abroad.

It is also possible to collect reward points, travel miles, or cash back. But if you've been reading this book carefully, you already know that.

Secret 119: No-Fee ATM Card

Consider signing up for a no-fee ATM card, which will give you the freedom to withdraw money without having to worry about additional fees.

Bear in mind that you don't necessarily have to change banks to avoid ATM fees abroad, since many banks will waive them for checking account holders.

Just beware that even if your bank doesn't charge you for an ATM fee, the local bank or ATM operator may, but you will be saving money nonetheless.

Secret 120: Cold, Hard Cash

It may be a thing of personal preference, but some travelers only use cash. Best of all, sometimes they don't have to worry about exchanging it for the local currency.

For example, American travelers often don't exchange dollars, since USD is one of the strongest currencies. This helps them avoid the fees they would otherwise have to pay for exchanging currencies. On top of that, the vast majority of vendors will give a fair exchange rate for a conversion from the US dollar to their local currency.

Secret 121: Find the Best Discounts

Trying to hunt down coupons or promo codes can be extremely exhausting and time-consuming. Sometimes they've already expired, or they never worked at all and just wasted your time for nothing.

But what if I told you that you could get coupons and promo codes automatically as soon as they appear?

Honey is a web browser extension with a database of thousands of different coupons and promo codes. When Honey detects a purchase that you could be saving money on, it automatically sends you the code and gives you a discount. The service is free and works for almost anything you can buy online, including plane tickets, hotel reservations, travel accessories, and so on.

Moreover, it has been recommended by *Time* magazine and *Business Insider*. I recommend it because the service is not only free and reliable, but it also saves you money and time. With it, I've been able to save money so many times for purchases I never expected I could save on.

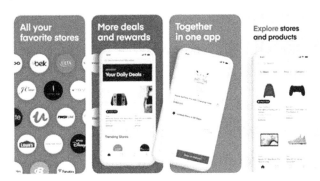

Visit: https://www.joinhoney.com/.

Secret 122: Mint

Mint connects to your checking and savings accounts, credit cards, and other financial accounts to help you organize your finances. With it, you can keep an eye on your travel budget and track your expenses during your trip.

The app is safe and widely used by many people, but unfortunately, it only works with American financial accounts.

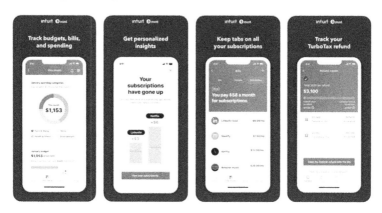

Visit: https://www.mint.com/.

Secret 123: YNAB (You Need A Budget)

My personal favorite money management (budget) app is YNAB, which is short for You Need A Budget. I use it for my daily life, and I love it because it helps you get ahead of your expenses. This means that you can also plan for a trip and start saving well in advance. In fact, you can create categories for the different parts of your trip, and you can book when you reach the goal for that item. For example, say you want to save $1,000 for the hotel, $500 for the flights, and $500 for meals and activities. You can set those specific goals and the day by which you want to have that amount of money, and the app will automatically tell you how much to save per month and help you keep track of it.

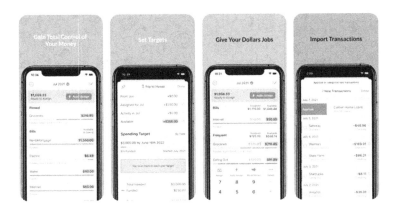

Visit: https://www.ynab.com.

Secret 124: XE Currency Converter

Not sure how to convert foreign currency when buying something? The XE Currency app gives you up-to-date currency rates, lets you convert different currencies, and can work offline as well. This way, you don't need to spend time doing brain-wracking math every time you try to buy something during your trip.

Visit: https://www.xe.com/currencyconverter/.

Secret 125: Splitwise

When traveling in a group, it's normal to share some of the expenses with your fellow travelers. Splitwise is an app that allows you keep tabs on all the shared expenses of the trip before, during, and after the trip. Then, it helps you settle all those small "debts" between you and your friends or family who are traveling with you.

The app is free and easy to use. It even lets you assign an expense to select members of your group or to all and then automatically keeps tabs on who owes who. It's pretty awesome to see it in action.

I've been using it for a couple of years now, and it has been great for group travel.

Visit: https://www.splitwise.com/.

Secret 126: Wise

If you're traveling to another country, sometimes you have to make a transfer to a foreign bank account. The problem is that most banks make that process much more complicated than it has to be and also charge you expensive fees.

The Wise app helps you make international transfers quickly and easily. They accept transfers to a variety of different currencies and countries, and their fees are also cheaper than most banks' and similar services' such as Western Union.

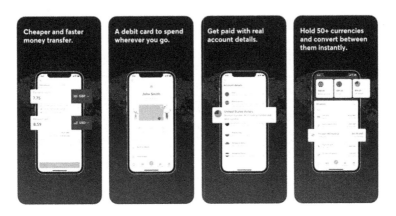

Visit: https://wise.com/.

Secret 127: GlobeTips

When eating in a foreign country, you may not be sure how to tip properly. The GlobeTips app shows how much to tip in more than thirty countries. It also offers a tip calculator for you to calculate the tip easily and quickly, as well as some tips on how to split the bill between you and your friends.

Cracking the Code on Travel

Part 16: How to Earn During Your Trips

Some people would love to travel long-term, but they just can't afford it because they haven't saved up large amounts of money.

However, thanks to the internet and other solutions, they can work while traveling and extend their trip for months or even years. Here are some of the possible sources of income you could use to fund your travels.

Secret 128: Teach a Language

Jobs that involve teaching a language are actually very common around the world and relatively easy to get if you know enough about the language you want to teach. Getting such a job is especially easy for native English speakers.

You can either get a job at a language school or give private lessons and charge by the hour. If you're interested in teaching English online, take a shot with some of these companies:

- iTutorGroup

- Gogokid

- DaDa

On some of these platforms, you can earn as much as $25 per hour and use the money to increase your budget and even extend your trip. However, you should note that most of these companies prefer hiring native English speakers.

Secret 129: Freelance Websites

Freelance websites have been very popular lately because they allow you to work from anywhere in the world over the internet. The most popular and respected freelance website at the moment is Upwork, while other popular platforms include the following:

– Fiverr

– Freelancer

– PeoplePerHour

– Toptal

– 99Designs

Secret 130: Be an Au Pair

If you enjoy taking care of kids and don't mind babysitting, then being an au pair could be your dream job. An au pair takes care of other people's children and is provided with room, board, and a weekly paycheck.

This kind of job is usually pretty time-consuming, but if you're well-organized, it still leaves enough time for you to explore the place you're visiting.

There are several websites that will help connect you with a family looking for an au pair:

- AuPair

- AuPairWorld

- Go Au Pair

Secret 131: Work at a Hostel

If you only need a free room and board, you could also work at a hostel. Hostels are always looking for someone to work at the front desk or show their guests around the city.

You can stay in these jobs for as long as you want, and for a couple of hours of daily work, you can get a free night to stay at the hostel. To find such jobs, I recommend using the Worldpackers website.

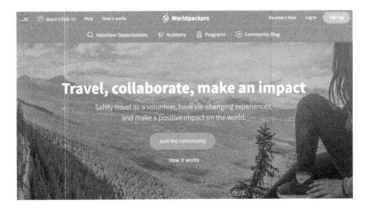

Travel by collaborating with hosts

Thousands of volunteer positions for you to collaborate, learn, and get immersed in the local culture in more than 140 countries.

Visit: https://www.worldpackers.com/.

Secret 132: HelpX

HelpX is a place where you can find both paid work and volunteer opportunities abroad.

You can find farm stays, homestays, B&Bs, hostels, or even sailing boats that are always up for having volunteers stay with them short-term in exchange for food and accommodation. Trying this out can be adventurous, and that means you will take a lot of terrific memories from it.

Visit: https://www.helpx.net/.

Secret 133: WorkAway

This is a website that might come in handy when you're a long way from home looking to earn some cash. It is similar to HelpX, but this website offers more paid job opportunities, as well as a few volunteer opportunities. Whatever your goal may be, it's worth looking at.

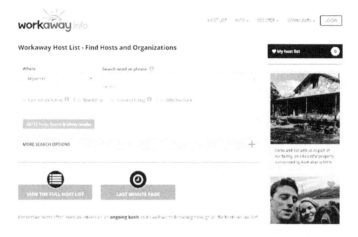

Visit: https://www.workaway.info/.

Secret 134: Grassroots Volunteering

Supporting and contributing to a good cause can sometimes be even better than having a job. If you like being kind and generous, you should check out Grassroots Volunteering.

The website compiles a list of ethical and responsible local volunteer organizations that keep the money within the community and not in the hands of big corporations. This is most certainly a great resource for anyone who wishes to volunteer while traveling.

Visit: http://grassrootsvolunteering.org/.

Conclusion

Congratulations, you have arrived at the end of this book, which was a journey in and of itself. I'm sure these tips will prove valuable to you and that you'll ask yourself, "How did I ever travel without these tricks?" every time you use one.

Now that you are ready for a new era in travel, I have to say this:

I'm so happy and proud that you'll now be able to travel a lot more for a lot less. I want you to spend less time planning and more time enjoying and creating amazing memories with your loved ones.

My fellow traveler, I'm sure that we'll meet somewhere while traveling – maybe on a beach or in the mountains. Who knows?

But wherever and whenever that happens, I hope you'll use this knowledge to go on trips you've never imagined to be possible.

Good luck and keep exploring!

David Adler

Made in the USA
Las Vegas, NV
17 October 2021